The Best of
UKRAINIAN CUISINE

The Hippocrene Cookbook Library

Afghan Food & Cookery
African Cooking, Best of Regional
Albanian Cooking, Best of
Alps, Cuisines of The
Aprovecho: A Mexican-American
   Border Cookbook
Argentina Cooks!, *Exp. Ed.*
Austrian Cuisine, Best of, *Exp. Ed.*
Bolivian Kitchen, My Mother's
Brazil: A Culinary Journey
Burma, Flavors of
Cajun Women, Cooking with
Calabria, Cucina di
Caucasus Mountains, Cuisines of the
Chile, Tasting
Colombian Cooking, Secrets of
Croatian Cooking, Best of, *Exp. Ed.*
Czech Cooking, Best of, *Exp. Ed.*
Danube, All Along The, *Exp. Ed.*
Dutch Cooking, Art of, *Exp. Ed.*
Egyptian Cooking
Filipino Food, Fine
Finnish Cooking, Best of
French Caribbean Cuisine
French Fashion, Cooking in the
   (Bilingual)
Germany, Spoonfuls of
Greek Cuisine, The Best of, *Exp. Ed.*
Gypsy Feast
Haiti, Taste of
Havana Cookbook, Old *(Bilingual)*
Hungarian Cookbook
Icelandic Food & Cookery
India, Flavorful (Gujarati)
Indian Spice Kitchen
International Dictionary of Gastronomy
Irish-Style, Feasting Galore
Italian Cuisine, Treasury of *(Bilingual)*
Japanese Home Cooking
Korean Cuisine, Best of
Laotian Cooking, Simple
Latvia, Taste of
Lithuanian Cooking, Art of

Macau, Taste of
Mayan Cooking
Middle Eastern Kitchen, The
Mongolian Cooking, Imperial
New Hampshire: from Farm to Kitchen
New Jersey Cookbook, Farms and Foods
   of the Garden State:
Norway, Tastes and Tales of
Persian Cooking, Art of
Pied Noir Cookbook: French
   Sephardic Cuisine
Poland's Gourmet Cuisine
Polish Cooking, Best of, *Exp. Ed.*
Polish Country Kitchen Cookbook
Polish Cuisine, Treasury of *(Bilingual)*
Polish Heritage Cookery, *Ill. Ed.*
Polish Traditions, Old
Portuguese Encounters, Cuisines of
Pyrenees, Tastes of
Quebec, Taste of
Rhine, All Along The
Romania, Taste of, *Exp. Ed.*
Russian Cooking, Best of, *Exp. Ed.*
Scandinavian Cooking, Best of
Scottish-Irish Pub and Hearth
   Cookbook
Sephardic Israeli Cuisine
Sicilian Feasts
Smorgasbord Cooking, Best of
South African Cookery, Traditional
South American Cookery, Art of
South Indian Cooking, Healthy
Sri Lanka, Exotic Tastes of
Swedish Kitchen, A
Swiss Cookbook, The
Syria, Taste of
Taiwanese Cuisine, Best of
Thai Cuisine, Best of Regional
Turkish Cuisine, Taste of
Ukrainian Cuisine, Best of, *Exp. Ed.*
Uzbek Cooking, Art of
Vietnamese Kitchen
Warsaw Cookbook, Old

The Best of UKRAINIAN CUISINE

Bohdan Zahny

HIPPOCRENE BOOKS
New York

Expanded paperback edition, 1998.
Third printing, 2005.
Copyright ©1994 by Bohdan Zahny.

Jacket design by Michael W. Yee.

For information, address:
HIPPOCRENE BOOKS, INC.
171 Madison Avenue
New York, NY 10016

Library of Congress Cataloging-in-Publication Data
Zahny, Bohdan.
The best of Ukrainian cuisine / by Bohdan Zahny.
     p.   cm.
Includes index.
ISBN 0-7818-0654-2
1. Cookery, Ukrainian. I. Title.
TX723.3.Z28   1994
641.5947'71—dc20   94-34724
                                                CIP

Printed in the United States of America.

CONTENTS

FOREWORD

This book presents both traditional and contemporary Ukrainian cuisine in an easy-to-use menu format. Ukrainian cuisine shares a common heritage with other regional cookeries, yet maintains its own unique character. Ukrainian food is universally known for its unforgettable taste, aroma, succulence and inventiveness.

Ukrainian dishes call for a variety of ingredients including natural products such as meat, poultry, fish, mushrooms, eggs, vegetables and fruits. Breakfasts are refreshing and nourishing, dinners usually of three courses, while suppers are light and mild. There is a great variety of soups and borsches in Ukrainian cuisine. Meat is usually seasoned with bay leaves, pepper and garlic and is served with side dishes and sauces. Ukrainians are fond of salads, cold and hot appetizers and starter courses as well as pancakes, dumplings and desserts.

Ukrainians use various ways of preparing their cuisine (frying, boiling, stewing and baking). The assortment of dishes includes the widely known borsch, as well as all sorts of *pampushky, halushky, vareniky*, stews, *pechiva* and numerous tasty drinks made of fruit and honey; altogether, these dishes will provide a great gourmet diversity for your table.

The main course at the Ukrainian table is usually a hot meat dish. The meat products most often used are pork, beef and poultry, though there are many veal and lamb dishes in Ukrainian cuisine as well. Meat can be prepared in a variety of ways but most often it is stewed. Some of the most popular Ukrainian dishes are jelly from pork leg, pork stewed with cabbage, chilled stuffed boiled pork, stuffed fried pork, Kiev style cutlets, home-fried meatballs (*bitky*), as well as meat casseroles and stuffed poultry.

The most favorite Ukrainian fish dish is crucian baked in sour cream. Also very popular are pike stewed with horseradish, carp stewed with onion or sour cream or stuffed with mushrooms and buckwheat, pike-perch baked with mushrooms and lobsters, fish roll-ups and similar dishes.

A variety of healthy and tasty dishes from grains is also an essential part of Ukrainian cuisine. Among them are *krupeniky*, buckwheat *bitky* and cutlets, *mamalygas, babkas*, sweet puddings, *kisiels* and various other sweet dishes. Groats, such as millet, farina, buckwheat, rice, oats, corn or barley, are as popular in Ukraine as in many neighboring countries. They are nourishing because they contain a lot of protein, mineral salts, carbohydrates and vitamin B, (especially buckwheat) and are gladly consumed by Ukrainians.

Dough products and pastry dishes are very popular at the Ukrainian table. For preparation of the dough, usually wheat, rye or buckwheat flour is used. Ukrainian pies made of pastry dough contain a variety of fillings, including meat, fish, farmer cheese, eggs, vegetables, fruits and berries. They are often decorated with assorted toppings and served at many occasions.

One cannot imagine a Ukrainian table without *halushky* or *vareniky* which are glorified in Gogol's stories. One can find here recipes for *vareniky* with cabbage, liver, poppy seed, plums and, of course, with sour cherries, as well as *halushky* with ham, potatoes or cream cheese. There is a variety of recipes for preparing pancakes of different kinds as well as *Ukrainian shuliky, potaptsy* or *hretchaniky* — dishes which are indispensable in Ukrainian cuisine. In the beverage section are several versions of *kvas* the popular fermented sour drink made of rye bread and water.

Ukrainans are known to be great sweet eaters. There is no Ukrainian dinner without sweet desserts. Sugared fresh fruits as well as fruits with sour cream and whipped cream are common. Different fruit and berry compotes, *kisiels* and vegetable and milk beverages are favorites. Fruits most often used for desserts are plums, apples, pears and apricots. The most popular berries are cherries, currants, strawberries, wild strawberries, and raspberries, often used in combination with honey and nuts.

The Ukrainian cuisine appeals to such a wide range of tastes and gourmet expectations that everybody is certain to find a favorite dish.

❈ APPETIZERS & SALADS ❈

UKRAINIAN STYLE EGG CROQUETS
ЯЄЧНІ КРОКЕТИ ПО-УКРАЇНСЬКИ

8 eggs, hard-boiled
½ c. flour
½ c. butter
2 c. milk
8 egg yolks
1 pinch salt
1 pinch gray pepper
4 T. bread crumbs

Peel hard-boiled eggs and finely chop them. Brown flour in butter in frying pan, slowly add milk and bring to boil. Combine chopped hard-boiled eggs, fresh egg yolks, salt and pepper; add to hot mixture; bring to boil. Cool. Make egg-shaped cutlets and roll them in bread crumbs. Serve with green salad.

LVIV STYLE CHEESE AND EGG APPETIZER
СИР З ЯЙЦЕМ

5 eggs, hard-boiled
½ lb. hard cheese
½ c. mayonnaise
1 T. chopped dill

Chop 4 hard-boiled eggs. Grate cheese and mix with chopped eggs. Season mixture with mayonnaise. Place on plate, decorate with remaining hard-boiled egg and chopped dill.

TOASTS WITH TOMATOES
ПОТАПЦЫ З ТОМАТАМИ

½ lb. thinly sliced firm bread
1 oz. butter
½ lb. large tomatoes
1 c. grated cheese

Brown bread in butter. Slice tomatoes and put one large circle of tomato on each piece of browned bread. Sprinkle with grated cheese. Warm in pre-heated 350° oven for 5 min.

MEAT SALAD
М'ЯСНИЙ САЛАТ

2 lbs. beef, veal or pork
6 eggs, hard-boiled
6 small pickles
3 onions
parsley and pepper
12 T. bouillon
1½ c. mayonnaise
1½ c. sour cream
salt and pepper to taste

Cook meat and cut into small cubes. Cube hard-boiled eggs and pickles; mix them. Peel and mince onions. Finely chop parsley and pepper. Combine all ingredients. Season to taste. Serve in salad bowl decorated with egg slices and green salad leaves.

11

MEAT AND VEGETABLE SALAD
М'ЯСНИЙ САЛАТ З БУРЯКАМИ ТА ГРИБАМИ

1 lb. beef fillet
¾ lb. cooked, diced ham
1 lb. beef tongue
4 beets
4 potatoes
¾ lb. pickled mushrooms
1 egg yolk
4 T. vinegar
1 T. sugar
6 T. olive oil
2 T. brown mustard
2 hard-boiled eggs for garnish

Cook beef for 35-45 min. and tongue for 30-40 min. until done. Cool and cut into small cubes and mix. Add diced ham. Peel, boil and cool potatoes; cut into cubes. Add boiled, cooled, peeled beets. Mix meat and vegetables well, add cut pickled mushrooms and half of vinegar. Prepare *egg-mustard sauce*: combine egg yolk thoroughly with sugar. Add mustard and salt, olive oil and vinegar alternately, beating constantly. Dress salad with prepared sauce, decorate with rounds of boiled eggs and serve.

TOMATOES WITH MAYONNAISE
ТОМАТИ ПІД МАЙОНЕЗОМ

4 tomatoes
1 T. fresh basil
½ c. mayonnaise
1 T. sunflower oil
salt and pepper to taste

Slice tomatoes. Chop fresh basil, add to tomatoes and toss well. Mix mayonnaise and oil and use as dressing.

CABBAGE SALAD
КАПУСТЯНИЙ САЛАТ

1 head of cabbage
1 c. mayonnaise
3 T. sugar
2 T. chopped fresh basil
1 T. lemon juice
3 T. chopped parsley
salt and pepper to taste

Chop cabbage; place in large bowl. Beat together mayonnaise, sugar, pepper, parsley, basil and lemon juice; add salt. Pour over cabbage and toss. Serve moderately cool.

CABBAGE SALAD KIEV STYLE
КИЇВСЬКИЙ КАПУСТЯНИЙ САЛАТ

½ head of cabbage
4 apples
1 carrot
1 T. lemon juice
2 T. crushed nuts
¼ lb. ground cheese
4 T. mayonnaise
3 T. sugar
3 T. chopped fresh parsley
1 T. chopped fresh basil
salt and pepper to taste

Cut cabbage into straws. Sprinkle with salt and mix well. Peel apples, quarter, core, cut into straws and mix with cut cabbage. Combine sugar and mayonnaise and toss thoroughly with cabbage mixture. Boil carrot, cool and cut into circles. Crush nuts. Grind cheese. Sprinkle salad with crushed nuts and ground cheese. Decorate with circles of carrot and finely chopped parsley and basil.

GROUND HERRING
МЕЛЕНИЙ ОСЕЛЕДЕЦЬ

3 herrings
3 onions
3 c. sour cream

Clean herrings. Remove bones. Cut fillets into small pieces. Grind them in meat grinder together with peeled onions. Add sour cream and stir well. Serve with pancakes as an appetizer.

HOME-MADE CAVIAR OF FRESH FISH
ІКРА ЗІ СВІЖОЇ РИБИ ДОМАШНЬОГО ПРИГОТУВАННЯ

½ c. caviar
1/3 t. salt and pepper
1 t. vinegar
1/3 onion
1½ T. oil
green parsley to taste

Remove caviar from the covering film and pour boiling water over. Let sit until the caviar turns white, then drain. Add salt and pepper, vinegar, finely chopped onion and oil. Mix well and let sit for 1 hr. Decorate with finely chopped green parsley.

HOME-MADE PIKE CAVIAR
ІКРА ЩУЧА

1 c. caviar
1 T. salt
3 scallions
1 t. vinegar
1 T. ground parsley

Take off the covering film and put caviar in a pot with cold salted water. Let it rest for 3-4 hrs. Drain off water. Add vinegar, finely chopped scallions and parsley. Decorate with a butter rose and serve.

KIEV STYLE HERRING
КИЇВСЬКИЙ ОСЕЛЕДЕЦЬ

½ lb. white bread
1 c. milk
1 herring
1 c. butter, melted
½ c. Holland cheese, grated
2 T. mustard
1 pinch pepper
1 pinch green parsley

Soak bread in milk. Squeeze it and grind with filleted herring in meat grinder. Drain the mixture. Add melted butter, grated cheese, mustard and pepper. Form into fish shape and decorate with sprigs of parsley and herring head.

MARINATED HERRING
ОСЕЛЕДЕЦЬ СВІЖОМАРИНОВАНИЙ

3 herrings
1 T. mustard
1 t. sugar
2 T. vinegar
1 T. sour cream
1 T. chopped marinated mushrooms
1 pickle, sliced
1 onion
¼ t. salt
4-5 slices lemon

Wash and clean salt herrings, saving milt. Cut off heads, fillet and soak. Stir milt with mustard, sugar and vinegar. Combine with sour cream and strain. Add marinated mushrooms, salt, diced pickles, and finely sliced onion, mix well and pour over the herrings on a plate. Cover and refrigerate for at least 3-4 hrs. Decorate with several slices of lemon and serve.

HERRING WITH SAUCE
ОСЕЛЕДЕЦЬ З ПІДЛИВОЮ

2 herrings
1 lb. white bread
2 c. milk
2 eggs, hard-boiled
1 T. vinegar
½ c. sour cream
1 T. mustard
1 t. parsley
2 pickles
2 tomatoes
2 onions

Cut filleted herring into small pieces. Mix with bread soaked in milk and grind in meat grinder. Arrange on serving plate in the shape of herring. Add the head and the tail. *For sauce:* mash egg yolks and add vinegar. Mix the batter with sour cream, mustard and salt. Pour over herring mixture. Chop boiled egg whites and mix with finely chopped parsley; sprinkle on herring. Decorate with sliced pickles, tomatoes and onions.

HERRING WITH APPLES
ОСЕЛЕДЕЦЬ З ЯБЛУКАМИ

2 herrings
2 c. cold water
4 apples
1/2 lb. white bread
2 T. butter
2 T. sour cream

Wash and clean fillets of herring. Soak in cold water for 2 hrs. Soak white bread in water; drain it. Wash and peel apples. Cut prepared herring and peeled apples finely. Mix with soaked and drained bread, sour cream and butter. Stir and arrange on serving plate in a shape of herring. Add the head and the tail.

ODESSA STYLE SHRIMP SALAD
САЛАТ ОДЕСЬКИЙ З МОРСЬКИМИ КРЕВЕТКАМИ

1 lb. shrimp
1 lemon
4-5 boiled potatoes
4 hard-boiled eggs
¼ lb. green peas, cooked
1 c. mayonnaise
salt to taste
salad greens

Clean, wash and cook shrimp, sprinkle them with lemon juice. Cut cooked potatoes and hard boiled eggs into slices, add green peas and shrimp (save a few for garnish); season with mayonnaise, salt, and mix gentley. Place in salad dish, decorate with greens, egg slices and peas.

SHREDDED BEETS
ТЕРТІ БУРЯКИ

1 ½ lb. beets
½ c. oil
5 onions, chopped and browned
½ c. tomato paste
3 T. sugar
1/8 t. black pepper
salt to taste
parsley for garnish

Wash and peel beets. Grate and sauté in oil. Add finely chopped and browned onion as well as tomato paste. Sprinkle with salt, sugar and pepper. Mix well and stew covered for 15 min. Cool, place on a serving dish and decorate with chopped parsley.

SALAD FROM BEETS AND HORSERADISH
САЛАТ БУРЯКОВИЙ З ХРІНОМ

¾ lbs. beets
1/8 t. cinnamon
¼ c. vinegar
½ c. sour cream
1 medium sized horseradish
salt and sugar to taste

Wash and bake beets. Peel and cut them into pieces. Add vinegar. Season with cinnamon and mix well. Place in serving bowl and pour over mixture of sour cream, grated horseradish, and sugar.

BEET AND MUSHROOM SALAD
САЛАТ БУРЯКОВИЙ З ГРИБАМИ

½ c. dried mushrooms
1 lb. beets
1 red onion
½ c. olive oil
¼ t. vinegar

Wash and soak mushrooms for 1-2 hrs. Cook them for 40 min. Drain and finely chop in straws. Wash and cook beets for 30-40 min. Cool and peel. Cut in straws. Mix with mushrooms. Decorate with sliced onion. Season with olive oil and vinegar mixture.

BUKOVINA SALAD
САЛАТ БУКОВИНА

1 lb. sausage, cooked
4-5 potatoes
2 carrots
3 green peppers
4 scallions
1 c. canned or cooked green beans
1/2 c. mayonnaise

Wash, cook and peel potatoes and carrots. Cut into cubes. Add cubed sausages. Mix with cut up green pepper, and scallions. Add green beans. Sprinkle with salt and stir well. Season with mayonnaise and serve.

SALAD WITH EGGS
САЛАТ З ЯЙЦЯМИ

1 lb. radishes
¼ lb. scallions
¾ c. sour cream
3 eggs, boiled
1 bunch dill
1/4 t. salt

Wash and cut radishes in circles. Mix with finely chopped scallions. Add salt and mix. Place in serving bowl. Season with sour cream. Decorate with quartered eggs. Sprinkle with finely chopped dill and serve.

SORREL AND SPINACH SALAD
САЛАТ ЗІ ЩАВЛЮ ТА ШПИНАТУ

½ lb. sorrel
½ lb. spinach
4 scallions
2 eggs
4 T. oil
1/4 t. salt

Wash and finely chop sorrel and spinach. Add chopped scallion and quartered boiled eggs. Mix well. Season with salt and oil.

FARMER CHEESE SALAD WITH VEGETABLES
СЕЛЯНСЬКИЙ САЛАТ ІЗ СИРОМ ТА ГОРОДИНОЮ

1 lb. farmer cheese
7 radishes
1 cucumber
2 scallions
3 T. sour cream
1/4 t. salt
1 t. sugar

Process farmer cheese through meat grinder. Finely cut radishes, cucumber and scallions. Mix with ground cheese. Add salt and sugar. Season with sour cream.

FARMER CHEESE APPETIZER WITH VEGETABLES
СЕЛЯНСЬКА СИРНА ЗАКУСКА З ГОРОДИНОЮ

1 lb. farmer cheese, grated
2 egg yolks, boiled and mashed
2 scallions
½ c. sour cream
2 tomatoes, radishes, scallions for garnish

Combine farmer cheese with egg yolks. Add finely chopped scallions and sour cream. Mix well. Transfer to serving dish and decorate with radishes, sliced tomatoes and finely chopped scallion.

MEZHIVO FROM EGGPLANTS
МЕЖИВО БАКЛАЖАННЕ

1 lb. eggplants
½ c. oil
2 onions
½ lb. tomatoes, sliced
1/8 t. gray pepper
2 bay leaves
salt to taste

Wash and peel eggplants, slice. Sprinkle with salt and set aside for 15 min; drain excess juice. Brown eggplant in oil until golden on both sides; brown onion and tomatoes. Transfer everything to stewing pan. Add cold water to cover, salt, pepper and bay leaf; stew for 15 min. Cool and serve.

SAUERKRAUT AND MUSHROOM SALAD
САЛАТ З КВАШЕНОЇ КАПУСТИ ТА ГРИБІВ

1 lb. sauerkraut
1 onion, chopped
¼ lb. marinated mushrooms
1 pinch cloves
1 pinch cinnamon
2 T. sugar
2 T. oil
3 T. chopped fresh parsley

Mix sauerkraut with chopped onion. Cut up salted or marinated mushrooms and mix with sauerkraut. Add cloves, cinnamon and sugar to oil and pour over. Serve with finely chopped fresh parsley.

23

CABBAGE, CARROT, PEPPER AND APPLE SALAD
САЛАТ З КАПУСТИ, МОРКВИ, ПЕРЦЮ ТА ЯБЛУК

1 lb. cabbage
1 carrot
¼ lb. green pepper
1/3 lb. apples
¼ c. lemon juice
½ t. salt
½ t. sugar
1 c. sour cream
3 T. chopped fresh parsley

Clean, wash and thinly cut cabbage; stir in salt. Drain and save as a healthy drink. Mix chopped cabbage with cut up carrot and pepper. Add peeled and cut-up apples sprinkled with lemon juice so that they will not darken. Combine sugar and sour cream, mix into salad and serve garnished with chopped parsley.

RED CABBAGE SALAD
САЛАТ З ЧЕРВОНОЇ КАПУСТИ

1 lb. red cabbage
2 T. vinegar
2 T. oil
2 T. sugar
¼ t. salt

Cut cleaned and washed cabbage and stir with salt. Add vinegar, oil, and sugar. Mix well and serve.

CABBAGE, APPLES AND ONION SALAD
САЛАТ З КАПУСТИ, ЯБЛУК ТА ЦИБУЛІ

> *1 lb. cabbage*
> *¼ lb. apples*
> *1 T. vinegar*
> *1 onion, chopped*
> *3 T. sugar*
> *¾ c. sour cream*
> *salt and pepper to taste*

Clean, wash and cut cabbage thinly. Peel and cut apples. Sprinkle them with vinegar so that they will not darken. Add chopped onion. Mix sour cream and sugar and pour over. Season with pepper and mix well. Serve.

CAULIFLOWER SALAD WITH BOILED EGGS
САЛАТ З ЦВІТНОЇ КАПУСТИ ТА ВАРЕНИХ ЯЄЦЬ

> *2 lbs. cauliflower*
> *1 T. vinegar*
> *2 T. oil*
> *1 T. sugar*
> *1 egg, hard-boiled*
> *2 scallions*
> *salt and pepper to taste*

Clean and wash cauliflower. Place in a pot with water and vinegar and let soak for 10-15 min. Drain and divide it into small pieces and wash again. Place in pot with hot salted water and cook for 20-25 min. Cool, dress with oil, vinegar, sugar and gray pepper. Add chopped boiled egg and finely chopped scallion, and then serve this exquisite dish.

CAULIFLOWER SALAD WITH TOMATO, CUCUMBER AND APPLE
САЛАТ З ЦВІТНОЇ КАПУСТИ, ПОМИДОРІВ, ОГІРКІВ ТА ЯБЛУК

1 lb. cauliflower
½ lb. apples
1 lb. tomatoes
1 cucumber
½ c. sour cream
1 T. vinegar
1 T. sugar
salt and pepper to taste

Clean, wash and cook cauliflower for 20 min. Cut cauliflower into small parts, add finely cut-up apples, tomatoes and cucumber. Stir well, adding sour cream mixed with vinegar, sugar and salt.

SALAD FROM GREEN PEPPER
САЛАТ З ПЕРЦЮ

1/3 lbs. green peppers
¼ t. salt
¼ c. mayonnaise

Wash, cut and clean green pepper. Cook in salted water for 10 min. Let cool and cut into straws. Stir in mayonnaise and serve.

RED CABBAGE SALAD WITH APPLES
САЛАТ З ЧЕРВОНОЇ КАПУСТИ ТА ЯБЛУК

1 lb. red cabbage
1 apple
2 T. vinegar
2 T. oil
2 T. sugar
1 pinch cinnamon
1 pinch cloves
salt to taste

Finely cut cleaned and washed red cabbage. Place in boiling water, bring to boil and drain. Add thinly sliced apples. Combine vinegar and oil and pour over. Sprinkle with sugar, salt, cinnamon and cloves; mix altogether and serve.

CARROT SALAD WITH APPLES
САЛАТ З МОРКВИ ТА ЯБЛУК

½ lb. carrots
¼ lb. apples
1 t. vinegar
4 T. sour cream
1 T. sugar
2 T. green parsley
salt to the taste

Wash and peel carrots and apples. Cut into thin slices. Pour over vinegar and sour cream combined with sugar. Sprinkle with salt and chopped parsley.

CARROT AND APPLE PUREE
МІШАНКА З МОРКВИ ТА ЯБЛУК

1 lb. carrots
1 lb. apples
8 oz. cream cheese
1 T. butter
1/3 c. sugar
2/3 c. sour cream or whipped cream

Cut peeled carrots and apples and brown in butter. Process through meat grinder. Stir in cream cheese. Add sugar and mix. Serve with sour cream or whipped cream.

BEET PUREE
БУРЯКОВА МІШАНКА

1 ½ lbs. beets
4 T. oil
2 onions
1 t. vinegar
1 pinch black pepper
3 t. sugar
1 t. ground cloves
1/8 t. cinnamon
1 pinch salt
1 bunch parsley

Wash beets. Bake in 350° oven for 30 min., then cook for 10-12 min. until tender. Peel beets, process through meat grinder, and brown in oil. Peel and cut onions; brown in oil. Combine beets and onions. Sprinkle with vinegar, black pepper, sugar, ground cloves, cinnamon and salt. Mix well. Place in serving dish and serve with finely chopped parsley.

UKRAINIAN ZAKUSKA
УКРАНСЬКА ЗАКУСКА

½ lb. beets, cooked
½ lb. cabbage
¼ lb. apples
1 T. salt
½ c. mayonnaise
1 lemon
½ lb. ham
½ lb. fillet of goose or turkey breast
2 eggs, boiled
2 cucumbers
3 tomatoes
1 bunch parsley

Cut peeled beets into straws, also cabbage and apples. Stir chopped cabbage with salt. Press out moisture and mix with cut apples and beets. Combine mayonnaise and juice of lemon and pour over. Add small pieces of ham and fillet of goose or turkey breast. Decorate with sliced eggs, cucumbers and tomatoes. Sprinkle with salt and chopped fresh parsley.

ASSORTED SALAD
САЛАТ-АСОРТІ

4 tomatoes
2 cucumbers
7 radishes
7 lettuce leaves
1 bunch parsley
¼ t. salt

Wash and cut tomatoes and cucumbers in half. Arrange alternately around edge of serving platter. In the center place radishes, lettuce and parsley. Salt and serve.

TOMATOES STUFFED WITH ONIONS
ТОМАТИ ФАРШОВАНИ ЦИБУЛЕЮ

2 lbs. tomatoes
3 onions
2 T. oil
¾ c. bread crumbs
1 T. chopped fresh parsley
1 pinch salt
1 pinch pepper

Wash tomatoes, core and remove 1/3 of pulp. Peel and finely chop onion; brown in oil. Add bread crumbs and finely chopped fresh parsley. Sprinkle with salt and pepper. Stir well. Fill tomatoes with prepared stuffing. Serve cold or warmed in 350° oven for 7-10 min.

TOMATOES STUFFED WITH CARROTS
ТОМАТИ ФАРШОВАНИ МОРКВОЮ

1 lb. tomatoes
¾ lb. carrots
½ c. sour cream
1 t. sugar
1 T. finely chopped parsley
pinch salt

Prepare tomatoes as above. Grate washed and peeled carrots. Combine with sour cream. Sprinkle with salt and sugar and mix well. Stuff tomatoes with carrot mixture and sprinkle tomatoes with finely chopped parsley before serving.

CUCUMBERS IN SOUR CREAM
ОГІРКІ З СМЕТАНОЮ

5 cucumbers
2 cooked egg yolks
½ c. sour cream
½ t. vinegar
1 pinch pepper
1 pinch salt

Wash, peel and slice cucumbers. Sprinkle with salt. Mash egg yolks with sour cream, vinegar, salt and black pepper. Pour over cucumbers and serve.

SALAD FROM SCALLIONS AND RADISHES
САЛАТ ЗІ ЦИБУЛІ ТА РЕДИСА

½ lb. scallions
1 bunch radishes
1 bunch dill
¼ t. salt
¼ c. sour cream
½ t. vinegar

Wash and chop scallions. Sprinkle with salt and stir with wooden spoon; set aside for 15 min.. Add cut radishes and finely chopped dill. Combine sour cream and vinegar. Pour over salad, mix well and serve.

SALAD FROM ONIONS AND CUCUMBERS
САЛАТ ЗІ ЦИБУЛІ ТА ОГІРКІВ

6 onions
3 cucumbers
1 T. oil
½ t. vinegar
1 t. sugar
1 pinch salt
1 bunch dill

Peel and cut onions into straws. Mix with peeled and sliced cucumbers. Place on serving plate. Pour combined oil and vinegar over them and sprinkle with sugar and finely chopped dill.

BOILED EGGS WITH HORSERADISH GRAVY
ВАРЕНІ ЯЙЦЯ З ХРОНОВОЮ ПІДЛИВОЮ

8 eggs
1 medium sized horseradish
2 T. butter
1 T. flour, browned
1 c. sour cream
1 t. vinegar
1 t. sugar
salt to taste

Boil eggs. Wash, peel and grate horseradish and brown in butter. Mix with browned flour. Add sour cream, vinegar, sugar and salt. Mix altogether well. Brown once again in butter. Cut peeled eggs in half and serve with this gravy.

STUFFED EGGS
ФАРШОВАНІ ЯЙЦЯ

10 eggs, boiled
3 T. butter
salt and pepper to taste

Cut boiled eggs into halves. Take out egg yolks. Mash throughly with salt and butter. Fill egg whites. Sprinkle with pepper and place on a serving dish. Serve with mayonnaise.

BORSCHES & SOUPS

UKRAINIAN BORSCH
УКРАЇНСЬКИЙ БОРЩ

1 lb. meat
1 parsley root
½ lb. beets
1 lb. potatoes
½ c. tomato paste
1 T. vinegar
1 T. pig fat
1 onion
1 T. flour, browned
1 lb. cabbage
1 garlic
1 T. butter
¼ t. black pepper
3 bay leaves
½ lb. tomatoes
½ c. sour cream

Cook meat in 2 qts. of water to make bouillon. Clean and shred parsley root and beets thinly in straws. Cut potatoes in cubes and place in pot with beets and sauté with tomato paste, vinegar and pig fat. Brown diced onion and parsley root. Mix with slightly browned flour, add bouillon and bring to boil. Place cut-up potatoes, cabbage and sautéed beets in bouillon. Salt to taste and cook 10-15 min. Add cubed meat browned with flour, bay leaves, black pepper and cook until potatoes and cabbage are tender. Add salted pig fat chopped with garlic to prepared borsch. Cut tomatoes, place in borsch, bring to boil. Cover borsch, when ready, and let it rest for 15-20 min. Serve with sour cream and chopped parsley.

POLTAVA BORSCH
ПОЛТАВСЬКИЙ БОРЩ

1 chicken
½ lb. beets
1 carrot
1 parsley root
1 lb. cabbage
1 lb. potatoes
2 T. vinegar
¼ c. tomato paste
1 onion
1 c. buckwheat flour
2 T. pig fat
1 T. butter
1 egg
1 green pepper
¼ c. sour cream

Cook chicken. Cut beets, carrots and parsley root into thin slices; cut potatoes and cabbage into cubes. Fry and stew beets with vinegar. Slightly brown carrot, root of parsley and onion and mix with tomato paste. Strain bouillon, add potatoes and cabbage and cook for 10-15 min. Add stewed beets, carrots, parsley and onion. Mix pig fat with green parsley, cook 7-10 min. and let "rest" for 15-20 min. Meanwhile boil ½ qts. of water for *halushky* (dumplings). While constantly stirring, pour in ½ c. of buckwheat flour. Take mixture off the heat and cool. Add an egg and the rest of the buckwheat and mix well. Drop batter by tablespoons into a pan of boiling water and cook until halushky rise. Put chicken and halushky into borsch and serve it with sour cream and finely chopped parsley.

KIEV-STYLE VEGETARIAN BORSCH
КИЇВСЬКИЙ ВЕГЕТАРІЯНСЬКИЙ БОРЩ

*¼ lb. fresh mushrooms or 2 c. dried mushrooms, re-
hydrated*
1¼ qt. beet bouillon or beet kvas
4 carrots
3 roots of parsley
4 onions, chopped, browned
½ lb. beets
1 lb. cabbage
1½ lb. potatoes
½ c. beans, cut up
1 lb. tomatoes
1½ c. sugar
salt to taste
½ stick butter
3 T. flour
½ c. sour-cream
2 egg yolks
3 t. green parsley

Cook mushrooms with carrots and parsley roots in bouillon. Add slightly browned onions and boil for 10 min. Remove mushrooms and chop. Strain bouillon into pot. Cut
up beets and cabbage in slices, and cut potatoes into
cubes. Cook beets in some of the mushroom bouillon until
tender. Cook potatoes, cabbage and beans in the rest of
bouillon for 10-12 min. Bring tomatoes to boil and crush
them. Combine bouillon with beets, chopped mushrooms,
crushed tomatoes, and slightly browned flour with the
potato and cabbage bouillon. Add sugar and salt and boil
for 7-10 min. Serve with sour cream, mixed with beaten
egg yolks and green parsley.

BORSCH WITH EGGPLANTS
ЧОРНО-СИНІЙ БОРЩ З БАКЛАЖАНАМИ

½ lb. beets
½ lb. potatoes
¼ lb. eggplants
½ lb. cabbage
2 green peppers
¼ lb. carrot
¼ c. tomatoes
¼ lb. onion
1 root of parsley
4 T. lard
2 qt. meat bouillon or water
1 T. tomato paste
3 bay leaves
1 T. sugar
½ t. salt
1 pinch gray pepper
1 T. green parsley
3 T. sour cream
1 T. dill

Cut up beets, potatoes, eggplants, cabbage, green pepper, carrots, tomatoes, onions and root of parsley. Fry and simmer beets with lard. Put potatoes and eggplants in meat bouillon. Bring to boil, add tomato paste and other vegitables and cook for 15 min. Add salt, sugar, pepper and bay leaves. Simmer an additional minute. Serve with sour cream, green parsley and dill.

KHERSON-STYLE BORSCH
ХЕРСОНСЬКИЙ БОРЩ

2-3 beets
3 c. water
½ c. cucumber slices
1/3 c. minced scallions
1 T. lemon juice & pulp
1 t. mild honey
2 t. fresh dill, chopped
½ t. crushed black pepper
½ t. salt
2 c. buttermilk

The Kherson borsch is a favorite summer dish in Southern Ukraine.
Wash and cut beets in 3 to 4 pieces each. Place in a pan with water, bring to a boil, cover, reduce heat and simmer 15 min. Turn off heat and cool. Slip beet skins off, and then grate beets coarsely or finely chop all the beets back into the water. Add thinly sliced cucumbers, scallions, lemon pulp, honey, chopped dill, pepper, and salt. Refrigerate. Stir in buttermilk before serving. Usually served cool; however, you can warm it before serving (do not bring to boil).

GREEN UKRAINIAN BORSCH
ЗЕЛЕНИЙ УКРАЇНСЬКИЙ БОРЩ

1 lb. beef
2 onions
3 bay leaves
1½ lbs. beets
2 T. vinegar
¾ c. tomato paste
2 T. sugar
1 c. chopped carrots
1 c. chopped celery
¼ c. flour
½ c. melted butter
2 ½ lbs. potatoes
1 lb. sorrel
2 bundles scallions
1 lb. spinach
2 T. chopped dill
1 T. lemon juice
½ c. sour cream
black pepper, salt to taste

Place meat in a pot, cover with cold water, add 1 peeled onion and bay leaves, sprinkle with salt, bring to boil, remove fat (do not discard) and simmer on very low heat. Cut beets into straws, place in separate pot with fat, sprinkle with salt, add vinegar, tomato paste, sugar and saute for 25-30 min. Wash carrots, celery and other onions, and cut them into straw, add flour and brown in melted butter. Add potatoes cut in wedges to boiling bouillon, along with stewed beets and browned vegetables and continue to simmer. When vegetables are almost tender, add finely chopped leaves of sorrel, spinach, scallions, bay leaf, and black pepper and thicken with white sauce (see Sauce section). Cut meat into portions and serve with sour cream and finely chopped dill.

CHORNYHIV STYLE BORSCH
ЧОРНІГІВСЬКИЙ БОРЩ

1 lb. beef
3 onions
1½ lbs. beets
6 T. vinegar
3 lbs. cabbage
1½ lbs. potatoes
½ lbs. squash
½ c. tomato paste
2 parsley roots
2 carrots
¼ lb. kidney
3 apples
3 tomatoes
½ c. lard
1 bunch dill
1 bunch green parsley
¾ c. sour cream
3 bay leaves
3 -5 peppercorns
salt and sugar to taste

Wash meat and place in a pot; cover with cold water, add peeled onion and salt and bring to boil. Skim off fat and reserve; continue simmering on low heat. Wash beets, cut into straws, sprinkle with salt, place in separate pot; add vinegar and stew in bouillon fat. Chop cabbage and salt it; cut potatoes into straws, and place cabbage and potatoes into boiling bouillon; simmer for 20 min. Add cubed squash and other vegetables, cut and browned in lard, cooked kidney, stewed beets, cubed apples, cut up tomatoes, parsley, bay leaves and peppercorns and simmer until done. Serve each a portion of meat with sour cream and chopped dill.

SMART BORSCH
РОЗУМНИЙ БОРЩ

1 lb. pork
1 lb. bones
3 onions
1½ lbs. beets
½ lemon
4 T. sugar
4 carrots
¾ c. tomato paste
2 ½ lbs. potatoes
2 lb. cabbage
¼ c. flour
½ c. lard
¾ qt. beet kvas
3-5 peppercorns
3-4 bay leaves
½ c. sour cream
salt to taste

Wash pork and bones and place in pot, covered with water; add 1 peeled onion and salt; bring to boil and simmer on a very low heat. Wash beets and place in a separate pot with cold water and juice of lemon; bring to boil and cook 30 min.. Remove from heat, cool, cut beets into straws and place in a pan with salt, sugar, beet bouillon and lard and stew covered until tender. Brown sliced onions and carrots in pork lard and tomato paste. Cut potatoes into wedges, place in the boiling bouillon and simmer for 7-10 min. Then add cut cabbage, stewed beets, browned roots, pepper and flour, season with salt, peppercorns and bay leaves and simmer until ready. Garnish with sour cream and serve with buns with peas seasoned with garlic or with warmed garlic bread.

VOLYN-STYLE BORSCH
ВОЛИНСЬКИЙ БОРЩ

2 lbs. beef
3 onions (medium size)
1½ lb. beets
4 lbs. cabbage
3 parsley roots
3 carrots
1 lb. tomatoes
¼ c. flour
½ c. lard
¾ c. sour cream
3 peppercorns
3 bay leaves
1 bunch dill
1 bunch parsley
salt to taste

Wash beef and place in a pan with salt and onion; cover with water and bring to boil. Wash and peel beets, place in a pot, cover with cold water, cook until half-done, cool, cut into straws and add salt. Brown sliced carrots, parsley roots and onion. In separate pot, simmer fresh tomatoes in lard, mix with browned roots and place in boiling bouillon; add beets and simmer borsch for 30-40 min. Season with bay leaves and peppercorns and simmer additional 5-10 min. Serve each plate with portion of meat, with sour cream, chopped green parsley and dill.

VOLYN-STYLE VEGETARIAN BORSCH
ВОЛИНСЬКИЙ ВЕГЕТАРІАНСЬКИЙ БОРЩ

1 c. dried mushrooms
3 onions (medium size)
1½ lbs. beets, cooked 30 min.
4 lbs. cabbage
3 parsley roots
3 carrots
¼ c. flour
½ c. lard
2/3 qts. beet kvas
3 bay leaves
¾ c. sour cream
1 bunch dill
salt to taste

Wash and soak dried mushrooms in cold water for 1 hr.; drain then cook with 1 onion for 30 min. on low heat. Cut half-cooked beets into straws. Finely chop cabbage. Brown roots and 2 onions with flour in lard. Combine all ingredients in boiling kvas, cook until tender; 3-5 min. before done, season with bay leaves and serve with sour cream and chopped dill.

HALYTSY-STYLE BORSCH
ГАЛИЦЬКИЙ БОРЩ

2 ½ lbs. beef bones
2 ½ lbs. beets
½ qt. beet kvas
1 c. tomato paste
4 carrots
3 parsley roots
4-5 onions
2 lbs. potatoes
2 ½ lbs. cabbage
3 bay leaves
3-5 peppercorns
¼ c. flour
½ c. butter
¾ c. sour cream
1 bunch dill
1 bunch parsley
salt to taste

Wash beef bones and cut beets into cubes; place in a stew pot, add beet kvas and stew with tomato paste. Peel and cut carrots, parsley and onion and brown them on low heat. Place finely cut potatoes and cabbage in meat bouillon and cook for 15 min. Add browned roots, season with bay leaf, peppercorns and salt and cook until ready. Cool for 30 min. Serve with sour cream, chopped dill and green parsley.

LVIV STYLE BORSCH
ЛЬВІВСЬКИЙ БОРЩ

2 ½ lbs. beef bones
4 onions (medium size)
2 ½ lbs. beets
3 T. vinegar
¾ c. tomato paste
3 potatoes
4 carrots
3 parsley roots
1 lb. sausages
1 stick of butter
5 T. sugar
¾ c. sour cream
3 peppercorns
3 bay leaves
1 bunch parsley
1 bunch dill
salt to taste

Wash and cover bones with water; simmer with 1 onion for 40 min. Wash unpeeled beets, cook in salted water with vinegar added; cool, peel, cut into straws and stew with tomato paste. Peel potatoes and cut in wedges; add to strained bouillon and bring to boil. Add browned sliced carrots, parsley and 3 onions. Season with salt, sugar, bay leaves and peppercorns and simmer until ready. Cool borsch for 30 min. while you cook sausage. Combine borsch with beet kvas and serve with cut-up sausage, sour cream and chopped dill and parsley.

BORSCH WITH KIDNEY
БОРЩ НИРКОВИЙ

2/3 qt. beet kvas
2 lbs. beets
½ lb. kidney
4 carrots, sliced
2 T. chopped parsley roots
4 onions, sliced
3 potatoes
1 lb. cabbage
3 T. vinegar
¾ c. tomato paste
¼ c. flour
1 stick of butter
3 T. lard
5 T. sugar
3 bay leaves
1/8 t. red pepper
½ c. white sauce
½ sour cream
1 bunch dill
1 bunch green parsley
salt to taste

Wash and cook beets for 30 min. in kvas and then simmer on low heat. In a separate pot cook kidney that has soaked in water overnight. Cut up roots and onion and brown in lard and tomato paste. Peel potato and cut into cubes, wash and chop cabbage. Take beets out of beet bouillon, cool and cut into wedges. Combine all vegetables, place in boiling beet bouillon and cook until ready. Add cooked kidney with cooking liquid to bouillon 5 min. before it is ready; season with vinegar, salt, sugar, bay leaves and red pepper; add white sauce and serve with sour cream and chopped parsley and dill.

BORSCH WITH MUSHROOMS & PLUMS
БОРЩ З ГРИБАМИ ТА СЛИВАМИ

½ lb. dried mushrooms
1½ lbs. beets
1½ c. tomato paste
4 onions
3 potatoes
2 ½ lbs. cabbage
3 parsley roots
5 carrots
¼ c. flour, browned
2 sticks butter
½ lb. dried plums
2-3 bay leaves
1/8 t. gray pepper
salt & red pepper to taste
1 bunch parsley, chopped
sour cream for garnish

Wash and soak dried mushrooms in cold water, cook in the same water for 40 min. Drain mushrooms reserving liquid and chop them finely. Place beets cut into straws in separate pan, add 1 cup of mushroom bouillon and tomato paste and stew until half-done. Brown chopped onion, carrot and parsley roots in butter; add browned flour. Place cut cabbage and potatoes in bouillon and bring to boil. Add washed dried plums, and all other ingredients to boiling borsch; season with bay leaf and pepper and cook until ready. Serve with sour cream and chopped parsley.

BORSCH WITH SOUR APPLES
БОРЩ З КВАШЕНИМИ ЯБЛУКАМИ

1 lb. meat bones
2 onions (medium size)
2 potatoes
¾ lbs. beets
4 T. vinegar
1½ sticks butter
¾ lb. cabbage
1 lb. sour apples
3 parsley roots
3 T. flour
1 c. sour cream
bay leaf, parsley & salt to taste

Wash meat bones, add 1 peeled onion, cover with cold water, add salt, cook for 30 min., and simmer on low heat. In separate pot put potatoes cut into wedges and bring to boil. Stew beets in bouillon with vinegar and half of the butter. Cut cabbage and sour apples. Brown onion and flour in the rest of butter. Combine all ingredients in boiling bouillon, and cook for 20-30 min. Season with bay leaf and pepper. Serve with sour cream and chopped parsley.

BORSCH À LA HETMAN
ГЕТЬМАНСЬКИЙ БОРЩ

2 ½ lbs. beets
2 lbs. meaty beef ribs
5-6 onions
3 bay leaves
3 potatoes
2 lbs. cabbage
6 carrots
1 lb. kidneys, cooked
3 parsley roots
1 lb. eggplants
¼ c. flour
1 stick butter
1 c. sour cream
3 bay leaves
salt to taste

Wash beets and cook for 30-40 min. until half-ready, cool and slice. In a separate pot, place beef ribs, cover with cold water, add 1 onion, and bay leaf and bring to boil. Remove meat and cut into portions, strain bouillon, add salt, bring to boil again and place meat and beets in boiling bouillon and cook for 30-40 min. Add potatoes cut into wedges and chopped cabbage. Simmer for 10-15 min., adding browned carrots, parsley roots and remaning onions, cooked cut-up kidney, and eggplants, which have been grated and stewed in butter. Serve with sour cream and finely chopped dill and green parsley.

FARMER BORSCH
СЕЛЯНСЬКИЙ БОРЩ

3 lbs. lamb
¾ lbs. onion
1¾ lbs. beets
2½ lbs. cabbage
½ lb. potatoes
½ lb. kidney
1½ sticks butter
1 c. tomato paste
¾ qt. kvas
4-5 carrots
2 roots of parsley
3 T. lard
½ lbs. apples, cut-up
3 peppercorns
1 c. sour cream
1 bunch dill
bay leaves
salt to taste

Place washed lamb in pot with cold water; add 1 onion, cut-up beets and salt and bring to boil, then add chopped cabbage. Add cubed potato and cook 15 min. more. Stew kidney in butter, tomato paste and kvas. Brown roots and rest of onion; add apples, peppercorns, bay leaf and salt and cook until ready. Season with lard. Serve borsch with a piece of lamb, sour cream and finely chopped dill on every plate.

LEAN BORSCH WITH CRUCIANS
ХУДИЙ БОРЩ З КАРАСИКАМИ

¼ c. dried mushrooms
2 carrots
1 onion
5 green olives
2 bay leaves
1½ lbs. beets
½ lb. cabbage
1 onion
4 T. vinegar
½ c. flour
1 lb. crucians
2-3 peppercorns
1/8 stick butter
2 T. vinegar
1 bunch dill
¼ c. sour cream

Soak dried mushrooms in cold water for 1 hr. and cook in water with carrots, onion, pepper, olives and bay leaves. Add cut up and salted beets and cabbage, bring to boil and simmer for 25-30 min. Brown second onion with flour, add vinegar and place into bouillon. Coat fish pieces with flour and brown; place in bouillon for last 5 min. Season with chopped dill. Serve with sour cream.

COLD FARMER BORSCH
ХОЛОДНИЙ СЕЛЯНСЬКИЙ БОРЩ

1 lb. beets
3 T. vinegar
1 lb. potatoes
½ lb. dried apples, plums, cherries
½ lb. cucumbers
2 eggs
3 T. sugar
½ c. sour cream
½ bunch scallions
1 bunch dill
salt to taste

Bake beets in 325° oven for 40-45 min. Cool, peel, cut
into straws, sprinkle with vinegar and let sit for 2 hrs. in
large pot. Cook cubed potatoes. Wash and cook dried
apples, plums and cherries for 15 min. Mix potato and fruit
liquids and pour over marinated beets. Add cubed cucumbers and chopped boiled eggs, season with salt and sugar.
Serve with sour cream, chopped scallions and dill.

COLD BORSCH WITH KIDNEY
ХОЛОДНИЙ НИРКОВИЙ БОРЩ

1/3 lb. kidneys
1 lb. potatoes
1 lb. red peppers
1 c. tomato paste
6 T. vinegar
½ c. oil
1 lb. beets, peeled and sliced
4-5 carrots
2 roots of parsley
3 onions
2 T. flour
1 lb. cabbage
¾ qt. kvas
3 T. sugar
3 peppercorns
1 c. sour cream
1 bunch dill
1 bunch green parsley
salt to taste

Soak kidneys for 2 hrs., then cook them for 20 min. Cube potatoes and place in boiling water. Cook for 15 min. and add boiled kidney with liquid; cut red peppers into straws, stew with tomato paste, vinegar and oil, beets, roots and browned flour and transfer into pot with potato and cabbage. Add kvas and cook 5-7 min. more. Season with salt, sugar, peppercorn and bay leaf and cook until ready. Serve cooled with sour cream and finely chopped dill every serving plate.

COLD BORSCH WITH KIDNEY ANOTHER WAY
ХОЛОДНИЙ НИРКОВИЙ БОРЩ ПО-ІНШОМУ

¼ *lb. kidneys*
½ *lb. beets*
1 *T. vinegar*
½ *lb. potatoes*
¼ *lb. cabbage*
1½ *qts. kvas*
2 *eggs, hard-boiled*
½ *bunch scallions*
1 *bunch dill*
2 *T. sugar*
½ *c. sour cream*
salt to taste

Soak kidney in water overnight. Cook unpeeled beets with vinegar, then cool and peel them, cut into cubes and add salt. Peel and cook potato, cut into straws. Cook cabbage in salted water and cut into straws. Cook kidney. Combine prepared vegetables and kidney in a pot with kvas, add finely chopped egg whites, scallion, dill, season with boiled egg yolks stirred with sugar, sprinkle with salt. Serve with sour cream.

SIMPLE BORSCH
ПРОСТЕНЬКИЙ БОРЩ

1 sliced onion
1 c. chopped celery
3 lbs. beets, peeled and cut
1/8 t. salt
½ c. sugar
1 egg
2 T. chopped dill
¼ c. sour cream
3 qt. water
1 T. lemon juice

Put onion, celery and beets in boiling water. Cover and simmer for 30-40 min. Add salt and sugar. Beat egg into 1 c. of the hot liquid and add slowly to the rest of the borsch. Sprinkle with dill. Serve with sour cream; hot in winter, refrigerated in summer. Yields 8-9 servings.

SOUP "THE SIMPLE ONE"
ПРОСТЕНЬКА ЮШКА

3 small white potatoes
3 carrots
2 lbs. ribs, cut in pieces
1 c. sliced white mushrooms
1 chopped onion
4 diced celery sticks
½ c. whole barley
½ c. white beans
½ c. peas
½ t. salt
1/8 t. crushed black or gray pepper
4 quarts water

Chop carrots and potatoes, and put in a kettle with water. Bring to boil and add all ingredients. Cover. Simmer for an hour and a half. Serve hot. Yields 10 servings.

POLTAVA STYLE SOUP WITH HALUSHKAS
ПОЛТАВСЬКА ЮШКА З ГАЛУШКАМИ

½ c. water
1 c. flour
1 egg
3 qts. water
1 lb. potatoes
2 onions
1/6 lb. pork fat
salt to taste

Make halushkas from flour, water, and egg. Roll out prepared dough in 1-inch thick, rectangular-shaped pieces.
Place cubed potatoes in a pot with boiling water, cook for
5 min., add halushkas and cook for 20 min. more. Season
with salt, paprika and onions browned in pork fat.

CHICKEN SOUP
КУРЯЧА ЮШКА

4 pound hen or stewing chicken
2 c. chopped celery
2 T. chopped parsley
1 onion
2 chopped carrots
½ t. salt
1/3 t. crushed white pepper

Put chicken in a large pot, legs down. Cover with water
and bring to boil, then reduce heat. Add celery, some of
parsley, onion, carrots, and salt; cover and simmer 50 min.
Add pepper, simmer 10 more min. Remove bones, skin
and cut up large pieces of meat. Serve garnished with
parsley.

HETMAN SOUP
ГЕТЬМАНСЬКА ЮШКА

½ chicken
1 stick butter
½ lb. ham
1 /2 lb. lean beef
½ lb. veal
3 carrots
2 roots parsley
3 celery sticks
¼ lb. bread
1 egg yolk
½ c. sour cream
1½ qts. bouillon
salt to taste

Clean and wash chicken, detach bones. Make bouillon with chicken giblets and bones. Chop chicken meat with butter, ham, lean beef, veal, carrots, celery and parsley. Combine meat mixture with bread soaked in hot bouillon, Pass through meat grinder and mix in egg yolk combined with sour cream. Strain bouillon into mixture and warm on low heat for 5 min. Serve garnished with green parsley.

DNIPRO RIVER FISH SOUP
ДНІПРЯНСЬКА ЮШКА

1 lb. pike, or similar fish
2 onions
1 root parsley
½ lb. potatoes
2 T. salt pork
4 scallions
2 bay leaves
3 peppercorns
1/3 t. salt
1 root parsley

Clean and wash pike; remove gills and eyes. Cover with cold water and cook with onions and parsley roots. Strain bouillon, add potatoes cut in wedges, cook for 10 min.; add pieces of pike and cook for 30 min. more until fish is done. Season with scallions stirred with salt pork, add bay leaf, peppercorn, bring to boil. Serve with chopped parsley.

MILK SOUP WITH VEGETABLES
МОЛОЧНА ЮШКА З МОРКВОЮ ТА КАПУСТОЮ

1/3 lbs. cabbage
1½ lbs. potato
2 carrots
2 c. water
6 c. milk
2 t. butter
salt to taste

Wash cabbage. Clean and cut into squares. Peel potato and cut into cubes. Grate carrots. Combine all prepared vegetables and cook in water for 10 min. Add boiling milk and butter and simmer for 10-15 min. Serve hot.

MILK SOUP WITH CAULIFLOWER
МОЛОЧНА ЮШКА З ЦВЕТНОЮ КАПУСТОЮ

1 cauliflower
5 c. water
2 t. farina
3 c. milk
2 T. melted butter
salt to taste

Wash cauliflower. Cut into small pieces and cook in pot of water for 15 min. Remove cooked cauliflower and set aside. Lower heat under cauliflower bouillon and gradually pour in farina constantly stirring. Bring to boil and cook for 3-5 min. Add cooked cauliflower and pour in hot milk. Simmer for another 5-7 min. Sprinkle with salt and add butter before serving.

MEAT DISHES

HOME-MADE PORK SAUSAGE
КОВБАСА ДОМАШНЯ ЗІ СВИНИНИ

pork casings
2½ lbs. pork
1 lb. salt pork
7 cloves garlic
5 peppercorns
2 t. salt

Clean fat from pork guts and wash very well. Turn them inside out and wash again. Pour hot water over guts. Rub with salt. Rinse a few times and soak in cold water for 24 hrs. Cut pork meat and half the salt pork into small pieces. Grind the rest and mix in. Add chopped garlic. Season with ground peppercorns and salt. Stir everything well. Fill prepared guts. Refrigerate for 5 hrs. Prick sausage with a pin or toothpick in a few places and fry in lard and onion until it becomes reddish-brown. Serve with horseradish. For side dish use sauerkraut, cooked or fried potatoes, cooked or marinated beets, pickles or salad.

STUFFED PORK STOMACH
КЕНДЮХ ФАРШОВАНИЙ

1 lb. fat pork loin
½ lb. ham
2 eggs
2 onions
salt and pepper to taste
2 lb. pork stomach
¼ lb. salt pork, diced

Cut pork into small pieces. Mix with ground lean ham. Add raw eggs, finely chopped onion, salt and pepper. Clean and wash pork stomach and fill with prepared mixture. Sew closed, sprinkle with diced salt pork and bake for 40-50 min. at 375°.

ROLLED PORK FROM SHANKS
ЗАВИВАНЕЦЬ ЗІ СВИНЯЧОЇ ГОЛІНКИ

2 lbs. pig shank
1 onion
½ bud garlic
1 carrot
1 parsley root
2 bay leaves
3-4 peppercorns
salt and pepper to taste

Wash meat well. Make a cut and remove meat from bone in one piece. Sprinkle with salt and pepper. Roll up. Tie with string. Cover with water, and boil with cut-up onion, garlic, carrot and parsley root. Season with bay leaves, peppercorns and salt. Simmer 1½ hr. Remove meat rolls; drain, cover with inverted plate and weight down. Take off strings; slice *zavivanetz*. Transfer to serving dish and decorate with green parsley. Serve with horseradish.

SLICED MEAT IN JELLY
ГОРОПКА ЗІ М'ЯСА

2 lbs. beef
1/3 lb. fat, cubed
1 lb. pork or beef leg
2 onions
2 carrots
1 parsley root
1 celery stalk
3 peppercorns
1 bay leaf
2 oz. gelatin per 1 cup bouillon
2 T. butter
salt and pepper to taste

Wash beef. Insert fat in slits cut with small knife. Brown meat in large kettle. Slash beef or pork leg in several places, brown. Cut up onions, carrots, parsley and celery and brown with meat. Add salt, peppercorns, bay leaf. Cover meat with bouillon or water. Simmer covered for 50-60 min. until tender. Detach bones from stewed meat. Strain cooking liquid. Add dissolved gelatin. Stir well and bring to boil. Cut stewed meat into thin slices. Transfer to bowl. Pour gelatin mixture over and set aside to chill.

PIG'S FEET JELLY
ТРЕМТЯНИЦЯ-ГОРОПКА ЗІ СВИНЯЧИХ НІЖОК

2 lbs. pig's feet
1 onion, cut up
½ bud of garlic
1 carrot
1 parsley root
2 bay leaves
3 peppercorns
½ t. gelatin
salt to taste
1 c. sour cream sauce
1 root horseredish, grated

Scorch pig's feet. Remove hooves. Slash, wash and cover with cold water. Bring to boil. Add onion, garlic, carrot and parsley root. Season with bay leaves, peppercorns and salt. Simmer for 60-70 min. Strain bouillon. Remove meat from bones and return meat to bouillon. Simmer for 15 min. more. Set aside. Dissolve gelatin in cold water. Combine with bouillon stirring constantly. Pour into serving dishes and chill for 24 hrs. Serve with sour cream sauce and grated horseradish.

PORK SLICES IN JELLY
ГОРОПКА ЗІ СВИНИНИ

1 small pig
1 onion
1 bud garlic
1 carrot
1 parsley root
3 bay leaves
5 peppercorns
2 t. gelatin
½ c. water
salt to taste

Scald pig. Scorch it, gut and wash it well. Cook covered with water in kettle with cut up onion, garlic, carrot and parsley root for 60-70 min. and season with bay leaf, peppercorns and salt. Remove pig and set aside bouillon. Cut pork into slices. Transfer to serving dish and decorate with slices of cooked carrots. Strain and boil bouillon for the second time. Combine with gelatin dissolved in cold water. Pour over the meat slices. Refrigerate for 3-4 hours. Serve with grated horseradish.

PORK ROLL
ЗАВИВАНЕЦЬ ЗІ СВИНИНИ

1 small pig (3 lbs.)
1 lb. pork
¼ lb. salt pork
6 eggs, hard-boiled
1 onion
½ bud garlic
1 carrot
1 parsley root
2 bay leaves
salt and pepper to taste

Scorch pig with boiling water. Gut, wash and slit up chest. Keep skin in one piece. Bone and cut off meat clinging to bones. Remove fillet and slice into pieces and grind all meat. Cut salt pork into cubes. Season with salt and ground pepper. Combine with chopped pork and mix well. Place half the prepared meat on pig skin. Place hard-boiled eggs cut into quarters on top of stuffing. Cover them with rest of meat. Roll up and place on a wet towel. Tie roll with string and transfer it from towel to pot of hot water. Sprinkle with salt. Add cut-up onion, garlic, carrot, parsley root. Season with bay leaves and peppercorns. Simmer 2 hrs. until done. Remove meat from pot, cover with inverted plate, and weight down until cool. Take off string before serving. Transfer to oval serving dish and decorate with green parsley. Cut meat-roll in pieces and serve with horseradish. A good side dish is boiled potatoes.

PORK ROLL POLTAVA-STYLE
ЗАВИВАНЕЦЬ ПОЛТАВЬСКИЙ ЗІ СВИНИНИ

1½ lb. pork
½ c. milk
1 bud garlic, minced
½ c. salt pork, diced
1 egg
salt and pepper to taste

Cut prepared and washed pork in pieces. Grind in meat grinder. Add some milk or water and grated garlic. Season with salt and pepper. Mix everything well and place on a wet towel. Spread and level ground meat. Sprinkle with diced salt pork. With help of towel roll up ground meat tightly and truss ends with towel to form a roll. Transfer pork roll into well-buttered baking pan. Brush with egg beaten with water and bake in pre-heated 375° oven for 1½ hrs. Drizzle with melted butter before serving. Serve hot or cool.

STEWED PORK FILLET
СВИНЯЧЕ М'ЯСО ТУШКОВАНЕ

2 lbs. pork fillet
2½ t. flour
2 T. lard
3 carrots
1 root of parsley
2 T. olive oil or butter
½ t. of black pepper
3 c. pork bouillon
10 grape leaves
½ bud garlic
4 lbs. potatoes
3 onions
1/3 t. saffron
3 T. chopped green parsley
salt to taste

Wash pork fillet thoroughly and dry. Add salt, dredge in flour and brown in hot lard. Combine with cubed carrots and parsley root. Brown in skillet for 8-10 min. Add ½ c. water. Sprinkle with a little pepper and stew for 10-12 min. Transfer to stewing pot. In skillet brown flour in olive oil. Pour over the pork stew with 2/3 of the bouillon and cover with grape leaves. Stew for 30-35 min. Remove grape leaves, sprinkle with salt. Add peeled and chopped garlic and stew for 10 more min. Cut potatoes and place in a separate pan. Add browned onion, sprinkle with saffron, pepper and salt. Pour over rest of bouillon and cook for 15-20 min. Serve mashed potatoes with sauce from the stew. Sprinkle with green parsley.

PORK RIBS STEWED WITH CABBAGE
СВИНЯЧІ РЕБРА ТУШКОВАНІ З КАПУСТОЮ

2 lbs. pork ribs
3 T. salt pork
2 onions, cut up
½ c. tomato paste
3 lbs. cabbage
1 T. vinegar
2 c. water
3 bay leaves
¼ c. sugar
salt and pepper to taste

Cut pork ribs into 2-rib pieces. Sprinkle with salt and pepper. Dredge in flour and brown in hot salt pork on both sides. Brown onion in pan's drippings. Add tomato paste and fry on low heat for 3-5 min. Transfer fried onion and pork to pot. Cover with water, and simmer covered on low heat for 40-50 min. Wash and finely cut cabbage. Sprinkle it with vinegar. Place in pot with 2 c. water and cook covered on low heat for 15 min. Combine stewed ribs and cabbage. Add sugar, salt, pepper and bay leaf. Mix well and stew for 20 min. more until meat and cabbage are ready.

PORK RIBS STEWED IN BEET KVAS
СВИНЯЧІ РЕБРА ТУШКОВАНІ У БУРЯКОВІМ КВАСІ

2 lbs. pork ribs
3 T. salt pork or butter
2 onions
2 T. flour
1 lb. beets
1 c. beet kvas or vinegar
1 bunch parsley
salt and pepper to taste

Cut pork ribs into small pieces. Fry in salt pork or butter. Sprinkle with flour. Add finely chopped onion. Brown meat on both sides for 5-7 min. Transfer to sauté pot. Add thinly cut beets. Pour over beet kvas. Sprinkle with salt. Simmer covered 50-60 min. until tender. Serve with finely chopped parsley.

STEWED PORK FILLET
СВИНИНА ТУШКОВАНА

2 lbs. pork
4 T. salt pork fat
2 c. vinegar or beet kvas
2 onions
4 green peppers
¼ lb. stale dark bread
salt to taste

Fry diced pork in salt pork on both sides. Transfer into sauté-pot. Pour over vinegar or beet kvas. Add chopped onion and green pepper. Sprinkle with salt and stew for 30 min. until half-ready. Add grated stale dark bread and stew 30-40 min. more until set.

STEWED PORK ZHYTOMYR-STYLE
СВИНИНА ЖИТОМИРСЬКА

2 lbs. pork
3 T. butter
2-3 T. tomato paste
1 c. mushrooms
1 lb. potatoes
1 carrot
1 onion
1 bay leaf
salt and pepper to taste

Cut pork into small pieces. Sprinkle with salt. Brown in butter on both sides. Stew 25-30 min. until half-done. Add tomato paste and stew for 30 min. more. Wash and cut up mushrooms. Cook in 2 c. water for 10 min. Set aside. Peel potatoes and carrot, cut up and brown in butter. Mix in chopped onion and season with salt and pepper. Place vegetables in stewing pot in layers alternated with pork. Add cooked mushrooms. Season with bay leaf. Pour over mushroom bouillon and stew for 10-15 min. more until ready.

STEWED PIG WITH HORSERADISH
ВАРЕНИЙ ПОРОСЯ З ХРІНОМ

pig (2-3 lb.)
½ lb. horseradish
1 T. flour
1 T. butter
2 T. vinegar
1 c. sour cream
2 c. bouillon

For side dish:
1 bunch fresh dill
2 lb. potatoes
½ c. sour cream
salt and pepper to taste

Clean and wash pig. Soak it in cold water for 2 hrs. Pat dry with towel and rub salt inside. Cook pig in unsalted water for 1½ hr. Remove pig and salt bouillon. Set it aside. Cut pig into pieces. Grate horseradish. Brown it slightly. Add pepper and vinegar and boil for 3-5 min. In pan slightly brown flour. Add pork bouillon and cook for 3-5 min. Add sour cream and simmer for 5 min. more. Combine with grated horseradish and cook for 10 min. Add butter. Serve horseradish gravy with pork. *For side dish*, serve boiled potatoes with sour cream mixed with finely chopped fresh dill.

STEWED PIG WITH HORSERADISH ANOTHER WAY
ВАРЕНИЙ ПОРОСЯ З ХРІНОМ ПО-ІНШОМУ

1 lb. pork
2 c. bouillon
1 T. flour
1 T. butter
3 roots horseradish
1 T. vinegar
1 c. sour cream
3 peppercorns
salt and pepper to taste

Place prepared pork in a pot. Add cold water, bring to boil and cook for 1 hr. Salt the bouillon. Cool cooked pig in it, remove and slice. *For gravy:* Grate horseradish, brown slightly in butter, add peppercorns and vinegar, bring to boil and simmer until liquid evaporates. Dissolve flour in bouillon, bring it to boil, add sour cream and salt, strain; combine with horseradish gravy, heat again and add butter. Serve with boiled potatoes.

STUFFED BAKED PORK
ФОРШОВАНИЙ ПОРОСЯ СМАЖЕНИЙ

1 pig
1 lb. veal
1 onion
1 carrot
2 T. butter
¼ lb. bread
2 eggs
½ bud garlic
1 bundle parsley
1 c. mayonnaise
salt and pepper to taste

Slit prepared pig along breast bone. Wash it. Remove all bones
except those of head and legs. Rub pig inside and outside with
salt and 3 cloves of crushed garlic. Let stand at room
temperature for 30 min. Remove veins, membrane and arteries
from pork's heart, liver, kidney and lungs. Wash them well
(especially kidney; best if soaked for 2 hrs.). Cook in salted
water. Set aside and cut in small pieces when cool. Combine with
washed and cut up veal; add cut up onion and carrot. Grind
twice in meat grinder. Add bread soaked in milk and egg yolks
stirred with butter. Sprinkle with salt and pepper. Moisten the
mixture with bouillon. Fold in whipped egg whites. Mix well and
stuff pig. Sew up with thread and place in roaster on rack with
legs pushed back. Cover ears and tail with aluminum foil. Roast
in 450° oven for 1½-2 hrs. When pig turns a light pink color, add
1 c. bouillon and baste every 15 min. with meat juice. Remove
from oven; pull out threads and remove foil. Transfer to serving
dish. Serve with mayonnaise and chopped parsley.

PORK FILLET STEWED WITH PLUMS
СВИНИНА ТУШКОВАНА З СЛИВАМИ

2 lbs. pork fillet
4 T. salt pork
1½ T. vinegar
3 peppercorns
2 bay leaves
4 c. water
½ lb. plums, pitted
4 T. bread crumbs
1 T. butter
½ c. sugar
2½ lbs. potatoes
salt and pepper to taste

Wash pork fillet. Sprinkle with salt. Brown in hot salt pork drippings until it turns a brownish-pink color on both sides. Transfer to stew pot. Add vinegar, peppercorns and bay leaves. Cover with water and simmer covered on low heat for 1½ hr. Cook washed and pitted plums. Process them and mix with bread crumbs browned in butter. Combine pitted plums with sugar and add drippings in which meat was stewed. Cook fruit sauce for 5 min. Bring to boil once more. Cube meat before serving and pour over plum sauce. Serve with fried potatoes.

PORK STEWED WITH POTATOES
ПОРОСЯ ТУШКОВАНЕ З КАРТОПЛЕЮ

2 lbs. pork
2 T. salt pork
2 T. flour
2 chopped onions
3 c. pork bouillon
2 lbs. potatoes
2 black peppercorns
2 bay leaves
1 T. chopped green parsley
salt and pepper to taste

Lightly brown salt pork in a frying pan. Add cubed pork, salt and fry with onion. Set aside half of onions, and transfer meat to stew pot. In frying pan brown flour in fat, add half of bouillon and bring to boil. Pour over meat in stew pot. Stew for 30-40 min. Add bay leaves, salt and pepper. Stew 15 min. more. Cut potatoes in cubes in another pan. Add browned onions, bay leaves, salt and pepper and rest of the bouillon. Simmer for 15-20 min. To serve place pork slices over potatoes. Pour over sauce from stewed pork and sprinkle with parsley.

MINCED BEEF CUTLETS
ЯЛОВИЧНЫ СІЧЕНИКИ

2 lbs. beef
3 onions
6 T. lard
6 eggs
3 T. crumbs
salt and pepper to taste

Pass meat through meat grinder. Peel onions. Cut into thin slices. Brown lightly in lard. Whip together raw eggs and pour over onions, cook till firm, constantly stirring. After chilling scrambled eggs, combine with meat. Mix well. Sprinkle with salt and pepper. Process through meat grinder. Form round or long patties about 1 inch thick. Roll in crumbs. Brown in hot lard on both sides. Transfer browned patties to baking pan. Add 2 T. of pan drippings, 2 T. of water. Bake covered in 325° oven for 12-15 min. Serve *setcheniki* with mashed potatoes sprinkled with finely chopped dill.

MINCED BEEF CUTLETS STUFFED WITH HORSERADISH
ЯЛОВИЧНЫ СІЧЕНИКИ ФАРШОВАНЕ ХРІНОМ

1 lb. beef
2 pieces white bread
½ c. milk
2 onions
4 T. butter
2 horseradish roots
2 c. sour cream
3 T. crumbs
salt and pepper to taste
1 lb. potatoes

Wash meat and cut into small pieces. Pass through meat grinder. Soak white bread in milk. Combine with meat. Finely cut and brown onion in butter. Add to mixture. Sprinkle with salt. Pass through meat grinder once more. Moisten hands. Make oval meat patties. Grate horseradish. Brown it in butter. Add 3 T. sour cream and mix well, and spoon in hollows in meat patties. Dredge in crumbs. Fry in butter until brown on both sides. Transfer to baking pan. Pour over rest of sour cream. Bake in 350° oven for 25-30 min. Serve cutlets and sour cream gravy with mashed potatoes.

COUNTRY-STYLE MEATBALLS
ЯЛОВИЧНЫ БИТКИ СЕЛЯНСЬКІ

2 lbs. beef
4 onions
2 T. bread crumbs
½ c. butter
¼ lb. dried mushrooms or
1½ lb. fresh mushrooms

Detach beef from bones, removing films and sinews. Wash, and grind meat. Mix with 2 peeled and finely chopped onions, and breadcrumbs. Sprinkle with salt and pepper. Mix ground meat well. Roll meat between palms forming 2 inch meatballs. Flatten "bitki" and dredge in flour. Brown on both sides in butter. Wash and soak dried mushrooms in cold water. Cook them in the same water for 30 min. until tender. Set aside. Drain mushrooms and save bouillon. Brown cooked mushrooms or fresh mushroms and chopped onion in butter. Chop 1 more onion. Place it in sauté-pot. Cover it with half of cooked and fried mushrooms. Place browned bitki on top. Then place the other fried onion and remaining portion of fried mushrooms on bitki. Pour over with mushroom bouillon and sauté covered for 10-15 min. For side-dish prepare potatoes sautéed in mushroom bouillon with tomato-paste and butter.

UKRAINIAN-STYLE PORK CHOPS
БИТКИ ПО-УКРАЇНЬСКОМУ З СВИНИНЫ

2 lbs. pork
½ lb. salt pork
4 onions
3 c. bouillon
¾ lb. rye bread
1 garlic bud
4 T. butter or lard
1 bunch parsley
salt and pepper to taste
2 lbs. potatoes

Cut prepared pork 1 inch thick. Pound to tenderize. Sprinkle with salt and pepper. Brown meat in salt pork. Chop and brown onion in butter. Place salt pork on the bottom of stew pan. Transfer browned pieces of pork to stew pan. Cover with browned onions. Pour over bouillon. Stew until done. Season with finely chopped garlic. Brown slices of rye bread in butter and transfer to serving plates. Place on each a slice of pork. Pour over drippings from stew pan. Sprinkle with chopped parsley. Serve with fried potatoes and pickles.

MEAT LOAF WITH SOUR CREAM
МЕЛЕНЕ ЯЛОВИЧНЕ М'ЯСО З СМЕТАНОЮ

2 lbs. beef
2 onions
½ lb. salt pork
2 T. flour
6 T. sour cream
2 c. water or bouillon
salt to taste

Pass prepared meat through meat grinder. Lightly fry cut salt pork with onion. Add ground meat. Brown this mixture. Add flour. Mix well. Pour over water or bouillon. Bring to boil. Simmer covered for 10-15 min. Transfer to serving dish. Season with sour cream and salt. Dress with mashed potatoes.

MINCED BEEF CUTLETS POLTAVA-STYLE
ЯЛОВИЧНЫ СІЧЕНИКИ ПОЛТАВСЬКИЕ

1½ lbs. beef
½ c. salt pork
1 clove garlic
2 T. bread crumbs
4 T. butter
2 lbs. potatoes
salt and pepper to taste

Wash meat and pass through meat grinder two times. Add chopped salt pork and garlic. Season with salt and pepper. Mix well. Add 2 T. water. Moisten hands and make oval cutlets. Roll them in crumbs. Fry in salt pork or butter until done. Serve with fried potatoes.

MEAT LOAF WITH CARROT AND SOUR CREAM
МЕЛЕНЕ ЯЛОВИЧНЕ М'ЯСО З МОРКВОЮ ТА ПІД СМЕТАНОЮ

2 lbs. beef
2 onions
2 carrots
4 T. butter
2 T. flour
4 T. tomato paste
2 c. water or bouillon
½ c. sour cream
salt to taste

Pass meat through meat grinder. Set aside. Wash and peel carrots and onions. Cut them into thin slices. Brown in pan with butter. Add ground meat. Sprinkle with flour. Mix well. Pour over bouillon. Add tomato paste and salt. Sauté until ready. Serve with sour cream.

MINCED BEEF CUTLETS ANOTHER WAY
ЯЛОВИЧНЫ СІЧЕНИКИ ПО-ІНШОМУ

2 lbs. beef
½ c. lard or salt pork
4 T. milk or water
2 T. pork fat
2 T. butter
salt and pepper to taste
parsley or dill

Grind meat with salt pork. Add salt, pepper and water or milk. Mix well. Make round cutlets 1 inch thick. Fry them in pan greased with pork fat until brown on both sides. Pour over melted butter. Sprinkle with finely chopped parsley or dill. Serve with fried potatoes.

BEEF SAUSAGE TCHERKASSY-STYLE
ЯЛОВИЧНА КОВБАСА ЧЕРКАСЬКА

1 lb. beef
2 onions
1 bud garlic, chopped
2 T. oil or fat
1 T. milk or water
1½ c. sour cream
1½ c. tomato sauce
2 lbs. potatoes
3 T. butter
salt and pepper to taste

Grind beef twice. Sprinkle with salt and pepper. Add browned onions and garlic. Pour over milk or water. Mix well and form into sausages 5-6 inches long and 1 inch thick. Transfer to pan. Fry until brown on both sides. Pour over sour cream and tomato sauce (see *Sauces & Gravies*). Bring to boiling. Serve with fried potatoes.

PEPPERS STUFFED WITH MEAT AND RICE
ПЕРЕЦЬ ФАРШОВАНИЙ М'ЯСОМ ТА РИСОМ

10 T. rice
2 lbs. beef
4 onions
6 T. butter
3 lbs. green peppers
2 c. water
3 tomatoes
parsley, salt and pepper to taste

For gravy:
4 T. flour
4 c. bouillon
4 T. butter
1 c. sour cream
4 T. tomato paste
parsley
salt to taste

Wash and cook rice for 7-10 min. Grind meat. Add chopped onions browned in butter. Combine with cooked rice. Sprinkle with salt and black pepper. Mix well for stuffing. Wash green peppers. Cut off their tops. Set them aside. Take out seeds and membranes. Cover with boiling water and let sit for 10 min. Drain them, stuff them with meat and rice. Close with their tops. Place upright next to each other in a baking dish, separating peppers from each other with tomato slices. *For gravy:* slightly brown flour. Add bouillon, sour cream and browned tomato paste. Sprinkle with salt. Mix well. Bring to boil and strain. Cover peppers with half the sauce. Bake peppers in 350° oven for 50 min. Serve with the rest of hot gravy sprinkled with thinly cut up parsley.

BEEF AND PORK CUTLETS STUFFED WITH BUCKWHEAT KASHA
М'ЯСНІ СІЧЕНИКИ З ГРЕЧАНОЮ КАШЕЮ

1 c. buckwheat
1 egg
2 c. water
4 T. lard or smaltz
1 lb. beef
1 lb. pork
1 c. milk
3 pieces wheat bread
4 T. butter
2 onions
salt and pepper to taste

For gravy:
1 c. sour cream
2 T. flour
3 c. meat bouillon
salt to taste

Brown buckwheat with one egg stirring constantly. Transfer to pot with hot water, add half the lard and cook for 7-10 min. Set aside. Cut and beef and pork into small pieces. Grind them. Soak bread in milk and drain excess. Stir it into ground meat. Sprinkle with salt and pepper. Grind the mixture in meat grinder once more. Add rest of lard and grated onion. Mix well. Form meat into oval patties. Make hollows in the center of each for 1 T. of buckwheat kasha. Reform meat patties and brown in butter. Combine ingredients fror gravy, pour over, and sauté for 15-20 min. (See recipe for gravy in *Sauces & Gravy*). Serve with boiled potatoes with melted butter.

MEATBALLS SAUTÉED IN TOMATOES
ЯЛОВИЧНЫ М'ЯСНІ ЧАВРИКИ У ТОМАТІ

1 lb. beef
1 egg
4 pieces wheat bread
5 t. milk or water
1 oz. leek or 1 onion
2 T. flour
1 T. tomato paste
2 T. lard (for frying)
1 c. bouillon
1 bay leaf
salt and pepper to taste

Grind meat in meat grinder. Add raw egg and bread
soaked in milk. Stir well. Add thinly cut and slightly
browned leek or onion. Mix thoroughly. Moisten hand and
roll meat between palms into meatballs 1½ inches in
diameter. Dredge in flour. Brown in lard until a light
brown color. Transfer meatballs to pot. Add tomato paste
and bouillon. Sprinkle with salt and pepper. Bake in 325°
oven for 20 minutes. Add bay leaf and cook for 5 more
min. Transfer to serving plate with sauce. Serve with
buckwheat kasha or mashed potatoes.

POTATO CAKES WITH MEAT
КАРТОПЛЯНИКИ З ЯЛОВИЧНИМ М'ЯСОМ

1 lb. beef
2 lbs. potatoes
1 egg
3 T. butter
¼ c. cream
2 T. flour
1 onion
3 T. olive oil
1½ c. mushroom sauce or 1 c. sour cream
salt and pepper to taste

Cook meat, wash, peel and boil potatoes. Grind boiled potatoes. Add raw egg, cream, melted butter, flour, salt and pepper. Mix well. Set aside. When meat is done, pass through meat grinder. Brown onion in butter. Mix it with meat. Pat out potato dough 1 inch thick and cut into 2-inch circles. Place into the center of each 1T. prepared ground meat. Shape into cakes. Fry in oil until brown on both sides. Serve with sour cream or mushroom sauce (see "Sauces").

STUFFED TOMATOES
ТОМАТИ ФАРШОВАНІ

10 tomatoes
1½ lb. beef
1 onion
2 T. rice, cooked
2 T. butter
1 T. bread crumbs
salt and pepper to taste

For gravy:
1 c. sour cream
2 T. flour, browned
2 T. butter
1 /2 c. tomato paste
salt and pepper to taste

Wash tomatoes. Slice off tops and set aside. Scoop out most of the pulp, and use for tomato sauce. Season prepared tomatoes with salt and pepper. Grind meat and add chopped and browned onion and rice. Season mixture with salt and pepper. Fill tomatoes with prepared stuffing. Close with tops and dredge in bread crumbs. Place on a generously greased baking sheet. Bake in 375° oven for 30-40 min. Serve with sauce made of sour cream mixed with flour browned in butter, tomato paste and pulp.

STUFFED CABBAGE
КАПУСТЯНІ ГОЛУБЦІ

1½ lb. cabbage head
1½ lbs. beef, cooked
4 T. rice
2 onions
3 T. butter
salt and pepper to taste

For gravy:
2½ c. bouillon
1 T. butter
1 T. flour, browned
½ c. sour cream

Remove outer leaves from head of cabbage. Wash them. Remove stem. Place cabbage in salted boiling water and simmer for 15 min. until half tender. Drain and set aside for 3-5 min. Separate leaves. Cut off thick parts. Sprinkle the leaves with salt and set aside. Grind meat. Cook rice for 5-7 min. until half done. Chop and brown onion in butter and combine it with rice. Season with pepper and salt. Mix well. Fill leaves with mixture. Fold in ends and roll up in rectangular packages. Transfer to baking pan. Combine gravy ingredients and pour over cabbage rolls. Bake in 375° oven for 1 hr.

ROLLED VEAL IN JELLY (ZAVIVANETS)
ТЕЛЯЗВО

2 lbs. veal leg
1/3 lb. liver
5 pieces wheat bread
1 c. milk
1 egg plus 2 egg whites
4 eggs, hard boiled
4 T. butter
2 carrots
1 onion
½ root parsley
1 oz. gelatin (per 2 c. veal bouillon)
salt and pepper to taste
1 bay leaf

Make long cut on veal leg. Detach bones and break them in small pieces. Scoop marrow out and chop up. Chop up liver as well. Set veal aside. Soak bread in milk. Combine it with chopped marrow and liver. Grind prepared mixture twice. Add 1 raw egg and melted butter. Sprinkle with pepper and salt. Cover gammon of veal thickly with stuffing. Place hard-boiled egg halves on top of stuffing. Tightly roll up meat and bind it with string. Put bones in pot and place meat on top of them. Add chopped carrot, onion and parsley. Sprinkle with salt and pepper. Cover with water and simmer covered on low heat for 1½ hrs. Add bay leaf. Cook for 20 min. more. Set aside for 5-7 min. Transfer cooked roll-up to board. Dissolve gelatin in warm bouillon. Add egg whites and mix well. Bring to boil. Remove from heat and set pan in cold water or refrigerate for 10-15 min. Cut meat thinly and arrange on plate. Decorate with bits of carrot, egg, parsley, etc. Pour over cooled jelly and refrigerate for 5-6 hours.

VEAL ROLLS
ТЕЛЯЧІ КРАПЛЕНИКИ

1 lb. veal
1 onion
2 T. butter or lard
¼ c. rice
2 eggs
½ c. flour
1 c. sour cream
½ c. bouillon
mushrooms
salt and pepper to taste

For stuffing:
1 onion
1 T. butter
salt and pepper to taste

Cut veal into thin slices. Pound them until very thin. Sprinkle with salt and pepper. Brown finely chopped onion in butter. Cook rice for 10-12 min. Mix cooked rice with browned onions. Boil eggs and chop them. Combine chopped hard boiled eggs with prepared stuffing. Season with salt and pepper. Divide the stuffing between the pieces of veal. Roll up and bind with strings. Sprinkle with flour. Brown on two sides in lard or butter. Transfer to sauté pot. Combine bouillon and sour cream, and pour over. Season with pepper and sauté for 40 min. until tender. Chop mushrooms and place in separate pot containing 1 c. water. Sprinkle with salt and simmer covered for 10-15 min. Serve veal with sautéed mushrooms.

VEAL WITH VEGETABLES
ОВОЧЕВЕ ТЕЛЯЗВО

2 lbs. veal breast, neck or shoulder
4 T. lard or butter
2 c. bouillon
3 carrots
2 roots parsley
1 onion
1½ lbs. potatoes
1 T. flour
1 c. sour cream
salt and pepper to taste
parsley or dill

Cut veal into small pieces and sprinkle with salt and pepper. Fry in lard or butter. When brown, pour over bouillon and simmer for 30 min. until half ready. Cut up and fry parsley root, potatoes, carrots and onions. Add salt and pepper. Add fried vegetables and sour cream stewed with flour to meat. Sauté 20-25 min. more until tender. Garnish with a little chopped parsley and/or dill.

VEAL WITH VEGETABLES
ANOTHER WAY
ОВОЧЕВЕ ТЕЛЯЗВО ПО-ІНШОМУ

2 lbs. veal breast
4 T. butter
3 onions
1½ lbs. potatoes
2 lbs. tomatoes
salt and pepper to taste

Wash veal breast. Place in baking pan. Sprinkle with salt. Dot with butter. Bake in 375° oven for 30 min. Peel and dice potatoes and onions. Brown separately in butter. Combine and season with salt and pepper. Cut up roasted meat and place in stewing pot under browned potatoes and onions. Add washed and cut up fresh tomatoes. Pour over meat drippings from roasting pan. Bake in 375° oven for 15 more min.

LAMB STEWED WITH PRUNES
ЯГНЯ ТУШКОВАНИЙ ЗІ СЛИВАМИ

2 lbs. lamb
1 onion
¼ c. flour
3 T. tomato paste
2 T. butter
½ lb. prunes
½ T. sugar
1 T. vinegar
4 c. meat bouillon
10 sweet cloves
1 pinch of cinnamon
dill, salt and pepper to taste

Cut lamb into small pieces. Sprinkle with salt. Fry in butter. Set aside. Brown finely chopped onion in butter. Stir in flour, tomato paste and 3 T. bouillon. Brown for 3-5 min. Return browned lamb to pot. Pour in 2 c. bouillon and stew 20-30 min. Add the rest of bouillon, as well as vinegar and fresh prunes. Season with cinnamon and sweet cloves. Stew for another 15-20 min. Sprinkle with chopped dill and serve.

COOKED LAMB WITH TOMATO SAUCE
ВАРЕНАЯ ЯГНЯ З ТОМАТНОЙ ПІДЛИВОЮ

2 lbs. lamb breast or shoulder
1 carrot
1 parsley root
1 T. butter
2 onions
1 garlic bud
2 c. tomato sauce
salt and pepper
1 bay leaf

Roast lamb for 1½ hours. Add peeled, washed and thickly cut carrots, parsley, onions, salt, pepper and bay leaves. Continue roasting for 30-45 min. more until meat is tender. (Do not overcook as meat loses its flavor.) Remove cooked meat, cut off bones and into pieces. Combine onion browned in butter and grated garlic stirred in salt to tomato sauce; pour over meat and stew for 10 min. Serve with boiled potatoes or buckwheat kasha as side dish.

LEG OF LAMB BAKED WITH KIDNEY BEANS
ЯГНЯ ПЕЧЕНЕ З КВАСОЛЕЮ

1 c. white kidney beans
2 lbs. leg of lamb
2 onions
salt and pepper to taste

Wash beans. Soak in cold water for 1 hr. Cook for 30 min. Mash and set aside. Wash lamb leg. Detach bones. Roast in 350° oven for 10-15 min. When it gives juice, sprinkle with salt and pepper. Continue roasting for 1-1½ hr. Peel and slice onions. Add onion rings to one side of baking lamb, and place cooked beans on the other. Roast for 15-20 min. more, basting with lamb juice and fat. Transfer to serving plate. Pour over juice from lamb and serve.

LAMB BAKED WITH KIDNEY BEANS ANOTHER WAY
ЯГНЯ З КВАСОЛЕЮ ПО-ІНШОМУ

1½ lbs. lamb
2 T. fat
1 c. kidney beans, cooked
½ c. sour cream
½ c. tomato paste sauce
2 T. bread crumbs
salt, sugar and pepper to taste

Wash lamb and sprinkle with salt and pepper. Brown on two sides in hot fat. Cut into pieces. Place in a deep skillet, well-greased with butter. Surround with cooked beans. Pour over sour cream and tomato paste sauce. Add sugar. Sprinkle with crumbs and dot with butter. Bake in covered skillet in 325° oven for 40-50 min. Serve with green salad.

LAMB STEWED WITH BEANS
ЯГНЯ ТУШКОВАННИЙ З КВАСОЛЕЮ

1 c. kidney beans
2 onions
½ c. tomato paste
2 T. salt pork or butter
¼ c. lard
2 lbs. lamb
½ bud garlic
1 T. flour
salt and pepper to taste
1 parsley root for garnish

Wash and soak beans in cold water. Cook for 30-40 min. Drain, reserving water. Brown peeled and thinly cut onion with butter. Add tomato paste. Brown for 4-5 minutes. Combine with water sieved from beans (1½ c.). Bring to boil. Add cooked beans. Sprinkle with salt. Bring back to boil and set aside. Wash lamb. Cut it into pieces. Remove bones and brown them in lard. Place in pot. Add 2 cups of water and sprinkle with salt. Bring to boil and simmer for 30 min. Rub pieces of lamb with crushed garlic. Stuff them with lard. Sprinkle with salt. Brown in salt pork or butter until light-brown crust is formed. Transfer to stewing pot. Pour over bouillon made of lamb bones to cover meat. Add lard and stew for 50-60 min. *For gravy:* lightly brown flour in butter. Add 1 c. bouillon, and salt and pepper. Simmer for 3-5 min. and strain. Pour gravy over meat. Bring it to boil. Drain cooked beans and add to meat and gravy; simmer and warm for 5 min. Serve lamb, cut up into small pieces, with cooked beans with gravy and thinly cut parsley.

STEWED LAMB RIBS
ЯГНЯЧА ТУШКОВАНА ГРУДИНА

1 ½ lbs. breast of lamb
2 T. salt pork
2 onions
3 carrots
1 root parsley
1 root celery
3 cloves of garlic
1 T. flour
1 T. butter
2 c. bouillon
1 bay leaf
salt and pepper to taste

Wash and cut lamb breast into pieces. Sprinkle with salt, pepper and flour. Brown on both sides in salt pork. Peel and cut up onions, carrots, parsley, garlic and celery. Sprinkle with salt and pepper. Add bay leaf. Mix and place in stew pot with browned lamb. Pour bouillon over to cover. Stew covered for about 1 hr. Serve with fried potatoes.

LAMB SAUTÉED WITH PLUMS
ЧВАНЕЦЬ ЯГНЯЧИЙ НАПІВТУШКОВАНИЙ ЗІ СЛИВАМИ

1 c. kidney beans
3-4 T. butter
2 onions
2 T. tomato paste
2 lbs. lamb
1 T. flour
2/3 lb. plums
10 cloves
½ t. cinnamon
2-3 bay leaves
1 T. vinegar
3½ c. bouillon
salt to taste
1 T. sugar

Soak beans in cold water. Cook for 20-30 min. Drain water and save. Brown one peeled and thinly cut onion in butter. Add half tomato paste. Fry for 4-5 minutes. Add water sieved from beans (1½ c.) and bring to boil, then add cooked beans, sprinkle with salt and warm up. Set aside. Wash and thinly slice lamb. Remove bones and brown them in butter. Transfer to pot. Add 2 cups of water. Sprinkle lamb slices with salt. Bring to boil and simmer for 30 min. Set aside. Sprinkle with salt. Fry in butter until golden on both sides. Transfer to stewing pot. Finely cut second onion and brown in butter. Add tomato paste and simmer for 3-5 min. Pour it over browned meat pieces. Add 2 c. bouillon made of fried bones. Stew for 30 min. Add washed and pitted plums. Dissolve browned flour in bouillon and pour over meat. Stew lamb for 50-60 min. adding the rest of bouillon when it is needed. Season with bay leaf, cinnamon, cloves and vinegar. Sprinkle with salt and sugar. Stew for 10-15 min. more. Arrange meat on platter with beans, stewed plums and gravy.

98

LAMB BAKED WITH VEGETABLES
ЧВАНЕЦЬ ЯГНЯЧИЙ ЗАПЕЧЕНЕ З ОВОЧАМИ
ЯГНЯЧЕ РАГУ

1½ lbs. lamb
2 T. salt pork or butter
3 T. tomato paste
1 T. flour
2 c. bouillon (or water)
7 potatoes
2 carrots
2 onions
1 parsley root
salt and pepper to taste

Wash lamb ribs (meat of neck or shoulders also can be used). Chop them up with bones into small pieces. Season with salt and pepper. Fry in hot salt pork. Transfer fried meat into stew pot and add tomato paste and slightly browned flour dissolved in bouillon. Stew for 50-60 min. until tender. Add fried potatoes cut in wedges, carrots, onions and parsley root. Mix well and bake in a covered pot in 350° oven for 25-35 min.

SAUTÉED LAMB WITH TOMATOES
ЯГНЯ ТУШКОВАНЕ З ТОМАТАМИ

1½ lbs. lamb
2 T. salt pork or butter
2 onions
3 T. tomato paste
2 cloves garlic
1 T. flour
2 T. bouillon
2 bay leaves
salt and pepper to taste

Wash ribs, neck or shoulder-blade of lamb. Cut up with bones into pieces. Sprinkle with salt and pepper. Fry in hot salt pork or butter. Shortly before it is ready, add slightly fried chopped onions and tomato paste. Sprinkle with rubbed garlic. Pour over water and stew. When it is almost ready, add browned flour, dissolved with bouillon. Season with pepper and bay leaves. Serve with mashed potatoes and gravy from stew.

LAMB COOKED WITH MILLET
ЯГНЯ ВАРЕНЕ З ПРОСОМ

1 lb. lamb
1 onion
1 c. millet
2 oz. lard
3 scallions
1 T. parsley
salt to taste

Cut prepared lamb leg or shoulder-blade into small pieces approx. 1-2 oz. each. Cover with water and cook with onion for 40 min. until half-ready. Add millet and continue cooking until lamb and millet are tender. Add lard and season with chopped scallion and parsley.

LAMB RIBS BAKED WITH RICE
ЯГНЯЧІ РЕБРА ЗАПЕЧЕНИ З РИСОМ

2½ lbs. lamb ribs
4 c. water
2 onions
1 carrot
1 parsley root
3 peppercorns
2 bay leaves
1 c. rice
2 c. bouillon
3 T. butter
2 cloves of garlic
sugar, salt and pepper to taste

Wash and cook ribs for 50 min. in water, adding cut up onions, carrot and parsley root; season with peppercorns and bay leaf. Remove lamb ribs from bouillon. Detach meat from bones and dice into small pieces. Mix with washed rice in casserole. Add 2 c. bouillon, butter, sugar and salt. Bring to boil. Transfer into 350° oven, cover and bake for 40 min. Serve with gravy made of browned flour, lamb bouillon, and seasoned with garlic.

MINCED LAMB CUTLETS
ЯГНЯЧІ СІЧЕНИКИ

1½ lbs. lamb
¼ lb. wheat bread
½ c. bouillon or water
2 egg yolks & 2 eggs
2 cloves of garlic
4 T. bread crumbs
2-3 T. salt pork or other fat
salt and pepper to taste

Cut up prepared lamb. Grind it. Add stale wheat bread soaked in bouillon or water. Grind together once again. Season with crushed garlic mixed with salt, pepper, and raw egg yolks. Mix everything well. Form cutlets. Dip into beaten eggs. Roll in bread crumbs. Fry in fat. Serve *sitcheniki* with fat in which they were fried with mashed potatoes.

PEPPER WITH LAMB STUFFING
ПЕРЕЦЬ ФАРШОВАНИЙ ЯГНЯЧИМ ШКРЯБОМ

4 T. rice
1 lb. green peppers
2/3 lb. lamb
1 onion
1 c. bouillon
1-2 T. butter
1½ c. sour cream sauce
2 T. chopped onion
salt and pepper to taste

Wash and parboil rice 15 min. Drain and set aside. Wash green peppers. Clean out insides. Place in salted boiling water for 2-3 min. Drain. Grind lamb twice. Add minced onion, salt, pepper and rice and mix everything together. Stuff peppers with lamb stuffing. Place in greased casserole. Pour over bouillon and bake in oven or on stove for 50-60 min. Combine sour cream and chopped onion and pour over peppers. Heat through. Serve hot.

POULTRY DISHES

YOUNG CHICKEN STUFFED WITH MUSHROOMS AND RICE
КУРЧА ФАРШОВАНА ГРИБАМИ ТА РИСОМ

1¼ lb. dried mushrooms
2 eggs
3½ T. butter
1 bunch parsley
¾ c. rice
salt and pepper to taste
2 lb. chicken
2 T. oil

For stuffing: Thinly slice cooked mushrooms. (Soak mushrooms for 1 hr., then cook in the same water for 25-30 min.). Sprinkle sliced mushrooms with salt and pepper. Add butter, raw eggs and parsley. Cook rice in mushroom bouillon until ready and mix with prepared mushrooms.

Gut, wash and salt chicken. Fill it with stuffing made of mushrooms and rice; place in casserole; add salt, oil and bake in 325° oven for 30-40 min. until tender. While baking, baste chicken every 5-6 min. with oil and juices. When serving, drizzle chicken with melted butter and sprinkle with thinly cut parsley.

CHICKEN JELLY
КУРЯЧА ГОРОПКА

1 medium chicken
6 c. water
1 onion
1 carrot
2 peppercorns
1 bay leaf
3 eggs, boiled
½ t. gelatin
salt to taste

Cut up prepared chicken; place in a pot; cover with water and cook for 2 hrs. Add cut up onion, carrot, bay leaf, peppercorns and salt. Simmer for 15 more min. Cut chicken into small pieces, place on a serving dish and decorate with sliced boiled eggs and pieces of boiled carrots. Pour over bouillon mixed with gelatin and refrigerate for 12 hrs.

CHICKEN PANCAKES
КУРЯЧІ МЛИНЦІ

1½ lbs. chicken
½ lb. stale bread
2 c. milk
2 eggs
3 T. butter
salt to taste

Remove meat from chicken breast and legs; add bread soaked in milk; pass through meat grinder. Add egg yolks and salt dissolved in milk; stir well and add beaten egg whites. Fry by spoonfuls in butter to a golden brown on both sides.

CHICKEN PIES WITH MUSHROOM STUFFING
КУРЯЧІ СОЛОНІ ТІСТЕЧКА З ГРИБАМИ

1½ lbs. chicken
2-3 oz. stale bread
¾ c. milk
1 egg
½ c. bread crumbs
3 T. butter
¼ lb. champignons or other mushrooms
2 T. sour cream
salt to taste

Grind chicken with stale bread soaked in milk. Add egg, salt, mix well and make small oval patties. *Prepare filling:* wash champignons. Cut them finely and sauté for 10-12 min. Add sour cream and salt, sauté for 10 more min., checking occasionally to see if the filling is thick. Cool, then place 1 t. mushrooms in the middle of each patty and cover with ground meat. Dredge in crumbs and brown on all sides in hot butter. Serve with green peas.

CHICKEN STEWED WITH DUMPLINGS
КОГУТИ ТРАДИЦІЙНІ

1 lb. chicken breasts
1 onion
1 carrot
3 T. butter
1 lb. flour
1 egg
4 c. water
salt to taste

Clean and wash chicken breasts. Cut into small pieces, salt and fry in butter until golden on both sides. Place in a sauté pot, add finely chopped onion and carrot cut in cubes; add water or bouillon and stew 1 hr. or so until tender. In bowl, stir egg and enough water into flour to form a stiff batter. Roll out 3/16 in. thick, cut into little squares, and cook covered for 10 min. in slightly salt boiling water or bouillon. Drain dumplings; rinse with hot water; place in with stewed chicken; season with butter and bake in 325° oven for 15 min.

TURKEY ROLL-UPS
ЗАВИВНЕЦЬ ІНДИКОВИЙ

5 lbs. turkey
1¾ lb. bread
2 c. milk
12 dried mushrooms (or 2 lb. champignons)
4 eggs
3 carrots
2 parsley roots
2 onions
4 c. bouillon
salt and pepper to taste

Cut cleaned turkey in half; take off bones. Cook bones for 30 min. Add heart and gizzard and simmer 30-40 more min. Fry liver with onion in butter. Soak bread in milk. Place turkey halves skin down, remove all meat from wings and legs, keeping skin in 2 pieces. Combine meat with bread soaked in milk and browned onion; mix well; grind in meat grinder, then stir well; add fresh eggs, salt, pepper; mix again and moisten in a small amount of bouillon. Spread the stuffing on the halves of the turkey-skin; roll them up; sew ends and tie with strong thread. Fry in butter to brown. Transfer to sauté pot; add cut carrots, parsley roots, reconstituted mushrooms, salt, and cover half way with bouillon. Bring to boil and simmer until turkey is done. Remove from bouillon, slice and serve with pan juices.

GOOSE WITH APPLES
ГУСКА З ЯБЛУКАМИ

1 goose
2-3 lbs. apples
1 bunch parsley
salt to taste

Clean, wash and salt goose; fill cavity with apple skins and cores, and bake in 350° oven for 2½ hrs., basting periodically until fork tender. When it is ready remove skins and cores; cut goose into pieces and serve with halves of apples baked separately in oven for 10-15 min. Season with finely chopped parsley and juice of goose.

STUFFED GOOSE
ГУСКА ФАРШОВАНА

1 goose
¼ lb. stale bread
1 c. milk
2 eggs
3 T. butter
3 t. bread crumbs
1 onion
1 bunch parsley
salt and pepper to taste

Clean and wash goose, rub inside and outside with salt. Let stand at room temperature for 1 hr. Grind bread, soaked in milk, and goose liver; add egg yolks, butter, salt, pepper, sautéed onion, finely chopped parsley, bread crumbs, and beaten egg whites and mix well. Fill goose with stuffing, not more than ¾ full, and sew up. Bake in pre-heated 350° oven for 1-1½ hr., periodically basting with juice.

STEWED DUCK
КАЧКА ВАРЕНА

1 duck
2 carrots
2 parsley roots
2 onions
1 c. sour cream
3 T. butter
bay leaf, salt and pepper to taste

Cut up cleaned and washed duck; salt well. Fry in pan for 45-60 min. until golden pink on all sides. Sprinkle with flour and fry for 10 min. more. Place fried duck in sauté pot; pour over hot water, add drippings from pan in which duck was fried, bay leaf, pepper, thinly chopped carrot, parsley and onion and stew 30 min. more until tender. Salt and season with sour cream. Serve with fried potatoes.

STUFFED ROAST DUCK WITH APPLES
ФАРШОВАНА КАЧКА З ЯБЛУКАМИ

1 duck
1 lb. apples, sour-sweet
1 T. butter
2 T. bread crumbs
2 lbs. beets, boiled
salt to taste

Clean, wash and rub duck with salt inside and outside. Wash and dry apples (do not cut them) and fill inside of duck with them. Sew up and roast in 450° oven for 10 min., then reduce to 350°, periodically basting with the pan liquid until golden on both sides. When it is fork tender, brush with butter and dredge with bread crumbs. Return to oven for 10-15 minutes until crumbs brown. Take apples out of duck before serving, cut it into pieces and garnish duck with cut baked apples and grated boiled beet.

ROAST DUCK WITH NOODLE AND MUSHROOM STUFFING
СМАЖЕНА КАЧКА З ЛАПШЕЮ ТА ГРИБАМИ

1 duck
3 T. butter
10 dried mushrooms or 1 lb. champignons
1 onion
½ lb. noodles
2 T. chopped fresh dill
2 eggs
2 c. mushroom bouillon
salt and pepper to taste

Clean, wash and sprinkle duck with salt inside and outside. Cook mushrooms, chop them finely and fry for 10 min. with chopped onion. Cook noodles in mushroom bouillon, drain, add salt as well as 2 beaten egg yolks. Fold in 2 egg whites beaten to a froth. Season with pepper and finely chopped fresh dill. Mix ingredients well and stuff duck with them, not more than ¾ full. Sew up, roast in 450° oven for 10 min., then reduce to 350° and periodically baste with the pan liquid until golden. Serve with mushroom gravy made of drippings from mushroom pan.

FISH DISHES

JELLIED PIKE
ГОРОПКА 3 СУДАКА

2½ lbs. pike, perch, or similar fish
1 carrot
1 root parsley
1 onion
2 bay leaves
3-4 peppercorns
2 T. gelatin
1 c. bouillon
5 boiled eggs
4 tomatoes
4 gherkins
salt to taste

Clean and scale pike trying not to damage skin. Remove eyes and gills. Wash well and place fish, with its belly side down, into a fish-poaching pot. Try not to bend fish. Cut up carrots, parsley and onion and mix with bay leaves, peppercorns and salt. Simmer in 7 c. water on low heat for 40 min. Set aside to cool. Remove fish and place it on a serving plate. Dissolve gelatin in a little bouillon, and then add it to the pot and bring it to boil. Add half the mashed hard-boiled egg whites to bouillon, stir well and bring to boil once again. Then add the rest of the egg whites and boil bouillon for 15 min. more to obtain a light color. Strain, cool and pour liquid over the pike. Refrigerate until set. Decorate with halves of tomatoes, boiled egg yolks and gherkins.

JELLIED UKRAINIAN PIKE
ГОРОПКА З СУДАКА УКРАЇНСЬКА

2½ lbs. pike, perch, or similar fish
1 onion
2 carrots
1 root parsley
1 celery stalk
3-4 black peppercorns
1 bay leaf
1 c. bouillon
1½ T. gelatin
1 root horseradish
1 bundle scallions
salt to taste

Cut up cleaned and filleted pike-perch into serving size portions and place them in a pot together with bones and fins. Add sliced onion, carrots, parsley and celery. Season with black peppercorns and bay leaf. Pour over 5 c. cold water, add salt and boil 30-40 min. on low heat. Transfer boiled fish to serving plate. Keep boiling bones and fins for 15 min. more. Strain bouillon. Add dissolved gelatin, grated horseradish and finely chopped onion. Pour over the fish on a serving plate. Cool and refrigerate for 5-6 hrs. until set.

PIKE ROULADE IN GELATIN
РИБ'ЯЧИЙ ЗАВИВАНЧИК В ГОРОПЦЕ

2 lbs. pike, perch, or similar fish
1 ¼ lbs. white bread
½ c. milk
2 T. butter
1 onion, chopped
1 egg
2 cloves garlic
½ root parsley
1 bunch green parsley
2 carrots
2 T. gelatin
½ c warm water
3 c. fish bouillon
½ t. salt

Clean and fillet pike-perch. Soak bread in milk. Brown onion in butter. Mix ingredients well, add egg, and grind in meat grinder. Add finely chopped garlic. Sprinkle with salt and pepper. Beat the mixture up and form into a roll. Wrap in cheesecloth. Tie in two or three places and at the two ends with a strong string. Transfer to pot with 5 c. salted water. Add chopped onion, parsley and carrots. Boil for 30-45 min. Take fish from bouillon. Dissolve gelatin in warm water. Add to bouillon and bring to boil. Set aside to cool. Carefully unwrap roulade and place it on a serving plate in a pool of jelly. Slice into portions and spoon over more gelatin. Top each piece with chopped parsley and with slices of boiled carrot. Cover with gelatin. Refrigerate until set.

ROLL-UPS FROM PIKE
РИБ'ЯЧИЙ ЗАВИВАНЕЦЬ

pike, perch, or similar fish (about 2 lbs.)
4 eggs, hard-boiled
2-3 bay leaves
1 onion
½ c. vinegar
1 bundle green parsley
sugar, salt and pepper to taste

For gravy:
5 egg yolks, hard-boiled and mashed
1½ c. sunflower oil
2 T. vinegar
1 t. mustard
1 t. sugar
1 T. round pickles
1 T. mushroom, marinaded
½ t. of salt
5 t. sour cream

Clean fish and cut in 4 fillets. Cover with finely chopped parsley and hard boiled eggs. Add salt and pepper. Roll up and tie with string. Boil gently in 5 c. water with vinegar, onion, bay leaves and pepper. Cool roll-ups in liquid for a while, slice and serve with gravy. *To make gravy:* beat together egg yolks, sunflower oil, vinegar, mustard with a pinch of salt and a pinch of sugar. When mixture is well mixed, add sliced pickles, marinated mushrooms and sour cream.

STURGEON SALAD
РИБ'ЯНКА СПЕЦ'ЯЛНАЯ

1½ lbs. sturgeon
8 hard-boiled eggs
½ lb. sardines in oil
¼ lb. butter
4-5 leaves lettuce or Chinese parsley
½ t. salt

For stuffing:
¼ lb. red caviar

Clean and wash sturgeon. Cook in hot salted water with onion on very low heat for 30-40 min. Put aside to cool. Cut cooked fish into 1 inch slices. Arrange around the outside of serving plate. Arrange sardines. Surround them by hard-boiled egg-whites filled with stuffing made of caviar with a dab of butter on top of filling. Melt the rest of the butter and pour over pieces of sturgeon. Decorate with lettuce or Chinese parsley and serve for very special occasion.

COD AND FARMER CHEESE PÂTÉ
ПАШТЕТ З ТРІСКИ З СЕЛЯНСЬКИМ СИРОМ

1-1½ lbs. cod
2-3 T. oil
1 onion
2 T. butter
¾ lb. farmer cheese (not sour)
5 blades scallion, chopped finely
salt and black pepper to taste

Wash and cook fillet of cod in cold water with onion for 30 min. Pass through meat grinder. Slightly brown cod and onion mixture. Sprinkle with salt. Grind everything a second time. Combine with grated farmer cheese. Add oil, sprinkle with salt and pepper and mix well. Place in well-greased casserole and bake in 350° oven for 30-40 min. Chill, add finely chopped scallion and serve.

PIKE SAUTÉED IN SOUR CREAM
ЗАЛИВНИЙ СУДАК СМАЖЕНИЙ В СМЕТАНІ

2½ lbs. pike, perch, or similar fish
2 lbs. potatoes
4 T. butter
2 c. sour cream
1 onion
1 carrot
1 parsley root
salt and pepper to taste

Remove fins and tail from fish. Scale. Wash fish well and slice into 2-inch steaks. Place in a baking dish, generously greased with butter: a layer of fish, a layer of sliced potatoes, one after another. Sprinkle with pepper and salt. Spread over carrots, onions and parsley, sour cream and melted butter. Bake covered in 400° oven for 35-40 min.

PIKE BAKED WITH MUSHROOMS AND LOBSTERS
СУДАК З ГРИБАМИ ТА РАКАМИ АБО ЛАНГУСТАМИ

1½ lbs. pike, perch, or similar fish
½ lb. mushrooms, marinated
10 portions of lobster
4 T. butter
4 T. crumbs
1 lemon
salt to taste

Remove fins and tail from fish. Scrape away scales. Wash fish well and slice into 2 inch steaks. Place them in pot. Simmer for 30 min. Set aside to cool. Remove bones, and transfer fish to baking pan. Place over them a layer of small marinated mushrooms, cleaned lobsters and their claws. Pour over melted butter. Bake in 375° oven for 45 min. Sprinkle with bread crumbs. Decorate with slices of lemon. Serve with potato balls.

PIKE WITH CHAMPIGNONS
СУДАК З ГРИБАМИ

1 carrot
1 parsley root
2½ lbs. pike, perch, or similar fish
½ lb. champignons
1 onion
1 bay leaf
3 peppercorns
½ lemon
3 T. vinegar
3 c. vegetable bouillon
3 T. butter
1 T. flour
salt to taste

Peel and cut up carrot and parsley. Transfer to pot. Pour over hot water. Add salt and cook for 15 min. Transfer to serving dish. Clean, wash and cut the fish into 1 inch steaks and place in stew pot. Pour vegetable bouillon over them. Season with peppercorns and bay leaf. Sprinkle with salt and simmer for 30 min. Transfer onto a serving dish. Squeeze lemon over fish. Wash and cut champignons in slices. Cover with a little water with vinegar added. Simmer on low heat for 5-7 min. Brown flour in butter. Add to simmering champignons. Add fish bouillon. Sprinkle with pepper and cook for 5 min. more until mushrooms are ready. As side dish use mashed potatoes and cooked carrot and parsley seasoned with mushroom gravy. Before serving, sprinkle with finely chopped parsley.

PIKE WITH DRIED MUSHROOMS
СУДАК З СУХИМИ ГРИБАМИ

1 c. dried mushrooms
2 lbs. potatoes
2 lbs. pike, perch, or similar fish
1 c. mushroom bouillon
2 onions
3 bay leaves
1 c. bread crumbs
salt and black pepper to taste

Wash dried mushrooms. Soak them in cold water for 30 min. Cook in the same water with added salt for 25-30 min. Wash and peel potatoes. Boil them in separate pot. Cut boiled potatoes into small pieces. Set them aside. Wash, clean and fillet fish; slice into 1 inch pieces. Finely chop mushrooms. Combine with cut fish and potatoes. Mix well and add slightly fried onion. Transfer to pot. Add bay leaf and pepper, mushroom bouillon and simmer for 20 min. on low heat. Roll fish in bread crumbs. Bake in 325° oven for 10 min. more. Serve hot. Use potatoes and mushrooms as side dish.

PIKE KIEVAN-STYLE
СУДАК ЗАПЕЧЕНИЙ КИЇВСЬКИЙ

1½ lbs. pike, perch, or similar fish
1½ lbs. potatoes
4 T. butter
2 c. mushroom sour cream sauce
1 oz. Holland cheese
5 eggs
1 bundle dill
salt and pepper to taste

Cut fillet into 3 inch pieces. Sprinkle them with salt and pepper and fry until golden on both sides. Boil potatoes. Cut boiled potatoes into rounds. Brown them in butter. Place fish on greased baking pan, decorate with browned boiled potatoes and pour over mushroom sour cream sauce. Sprinkle with grated cheese and melted butter; beat together eggs and pour over. Bake in 325° oven for 20 min. Decorate with chopped dill and serve.

FLOUNDER WITH MAYONNAISE
КАМБАЛА ПІД МАЙОНЕЗОМ

1-1½ lbs. flounder
5 potatoes
1 onion
3 eggs
2 cups mayonnaise
1 bundle dill
salt to taste

Wash and clean fish. Soak for 1 hr. Wash and peel potatoes. Boil them in salted water. Drain and keep potatoes warm. Transfer cleaned fish to pot with 5 c. cold water. Add onion and salt. Cook for 20-25 min. Set fish in broth to cool, then remove bones and skin. Transfer boiled potatoes to serving dish. Cut in quarters. Pour over 1 c. mayonnaise. Put fish over potatoes and cover over with the rest of mayonnaise. Decorate with segments of hard boiled eggs. Sprinkle with finely chopped dill and serve.

FISH BALLS FROM COD AND FARMER CHEESE
РИБ'ЯЧІ ТІФТЕЛЬКИ З ТРІСКИ ТА СЕЛЯНСЬКОГО СИРУ

1 lb. cod fillet
½ lb. white bread
1 c. water
1 onion
¾ lb. farmer cheese
2 T. butter
2 T. flour
2 T. tomato sauce
salt to taste

Wash fillet of cod. Cut into pieces and pass them through meat grinder. Add white bread soaked in water and chopped onion. Sprinkle with salt. Combine with grated cheese and mix well. Make small balls and roll them up in flour. Place in greased baking dish or casserole. Drizzle with melted butter and bake in 325° oven for 25-30 min. Serve with tomato sauce.

COD FILLET AND FARMER CHEESE CASSEROLE
ГАРЯЧІ ХРУСТЕЧКИ З ТРІСКИ ТА СЕЛЯНСЬКОГО СИРУ

1 lb. cod fillet
½ lb. farmer cheese
1 onion
5 carrots
2 T. oil
1 c. white sauce
2 T. butter
salt to taste

For white sauce:
½ c. flour
1 T. butter
1½ c. meat bouillon
1 onion
1 parsley root
1 celery
1 T. butter stalk
½ lemon

Wash fillet of cod and cut into pieces. Pass them through meat grinder. Add grated farmer cheese and slightly browned chopped onion. Grate and sauté carrots. Combine with 1 c. white sauce, sprinkle with salt, mix well with fish. Place the mixture in well-greased baking dish. Sprinkle with melted butter and bake in 325° oven for 25-30 min. Serve with melted butter and remaining white sauce (see in *Sauces and Gravies*).

CARP WITH HONEY
КОРОП З МЕДОМ

2 lbs. carp
1 carrot
1 onion
1 parsley root
1 bunch green parsley
1 lemon
2 eggs, hard boiled
2 T. gelatin
1 c. bouillon
1 T. vinegar
1 t. salt
2 T. sugar
black pepper to taste
3 T. horseradish
1 c. raisins
½ c. honey

Clean, scale and rinse carp. Cut off head and fins. Fillet fish. Slice cleaned and filleted carp into 2 inch steaks. Sprinkle them with salt and refrigerate for 50-60 min, then transfer to pot with cut up carrots, parsley and onion. Pour over 6 c. hot water. Add black pepper. Boil on low heat for 40 min. Strain bouillon into another pot. Arrange fish on serving plate and decorate every piece with slice of lemon, boiled egg and leaves of green parsley. Boil strained fish bouillon for 10-15 min. until it diminishes twice in volume. Set aside to cool. Add gelatin dissolved in a little fish bouillon and mix well. Pour in vinegar and boil again. In separate pot bring to boil raisins with honey. Strain bouillon and add raisins boiled with honey. Set aside and when it is chilled pour liquid over the fish. Refrigerate until set. Serve with horseradish.

CARP STEWED WITH ONION
КОРОП ТУШКОВАННИЙ З ЦИБУЛЕЮ

2 lbs. carp
2 T. flour
3 onions
4 T. oil
2-3 bay leaves
3 cloves garlic
3 peppercorns
¼ t. cloves
1 T. sugar
2 T. vinegar
salt and pepper to taste

Clean and scale carp. Rinse well. Remove head, fins and tail, and boil them with one onion in 5 c. water. Make a slit along backbone of fish and slice into 2 inch pieces. Sprinkle with salt and pepper. Roll in flour and then fry in oil. Peel and finely chop 2 onions. Brown in oil. Transfer half to pot. Add bay leaf, peppercorns, cloves, sugar and vinegar. Place fish on top. Sprinkle with the rest of the browned onion. Pour over fish bouillon, simmer on low heat for 30-40 min. Serve fish with stewing liquid and sprinkle it with green parsley. Serve with fried potatoes.

CARP WITH SOUR AND SWEET GRAVY
КОРОП ЗІ СМАЧНОЮ ПІДЛИВОЮ

1½ lbs. carp
1 onion
1 carrot
1 parsley root
1 bay leaf

For gravy:
1 t. flour
½ lemon
1½ c. bouillon
2 T. raisins
2 T. butter
2 T. tomato paste
4 t. sugar

Clean, scale and rinse carp. Cut off head and fins and boil in 5 c. water with onion. Slice fish into 1 inch steaks. Sprinkle with salt and refrigerate for 60 min. Chop onion, cut carrot, and parsley and place in pot with fish steaks on top. Pour over bouillon, add salt and bay leaf. Simmer for 40-50 min. on low heat. *For gravy:* brown flour, combine bouillon, tomato-paste sautéed with butter and juice squeezed from lemon. Mix well, boil and pour through sieve. Add raisins, simmer briefly. Stir in butter and sugar. Arrange steaks on platter, pour gravy over them, and serve with mashed potatoes.

CARP WITH BUCKWHEAT AND MUSHROOMS
КОРОП З ГРЕЧАНОЮ КАШЕЮ ТА ГРИБАМИ

2½ lbs. carp
1/8 oz. dried mushrooms
1 bay leaf
½ carrot
½ c. buckwheat (kasha)
2 onions
5 T. butter
3 eggs
2 T. flour
2 c. bouillon
3 sprigs parsley
salt and pepper to taste

Clean and rinse carp. Make a slit along spine, take out bones and guts. Sprinkle with salt and refrigerate for 50-60 min. *For filling:* soak mushrooms for 1 hour, cut up, and simmer in same water with 1 onion, carrot and bay leaf for 20 min. Strain mushroom bouillon and use it for cooking buckwheat kasha. Fry cooked mushrooms with chopped onion. Sprinkle with pepper and salt. Mix with buckwheat kasha, vegetables and eggs. Fill carp with stuffing. Sew up cavity. Roll stuffed fish in flour. Fry in butter until it is a golden color on both sides. Transfer to an oblong casserole and bake in 350° oven for 30-40 min. until fish is done. To serve slice and drizzle with melted butter, sprinkle with chopped parsley and accompany with sauerkraut.

CRUCIANS IN SOUR CREAM
КАРАСІ У СМЕТАНІ

1½ lbs. crucians, carp, or similar fish
1 t. pepper
2 T. flour
5 T. butter
2 lbs. potatoes
1½ c. sour cream
1 T. flour
1 T. crumbs
1 bunch dill
1 t. salt

Scale and clean crucians or calico bass. Remove guts and gills. Pat dry and rub with salt. Roll in flour. Fry to a crusty golden brown on both sides. Slice potatoes and fry in butter. Transfer browned fish to well greased pan. Arrange fried potatoes arround them. Blend sour cream with flour and salt and pour over fish. Sprinkle with crumbs. Drizzle with 2 T. melted butter. Bake covered in 350° oven for 30 min. until fish is done. Sprinkle with finely chopped dill. Serve with a salad.

TENCH WITH CABBAGE
ЛІНЬ З КАПУСТОЙ

2½ lbs. tench, or similar fish
1 t. pepper
1 egg
2 T. bread crumbs
5 T. oil
2 T. butter
½ c. dried mushrooms
1 cabbage (about 2 lbs.)
2 onions
½ t. ground cloves
pepper to taste
½ c. sour cream
1 bunch green parsley
4 t. sugar
1 t. cinnamon

Clean, fillet, slice and rinse tench. Sprinkle with salt and pepper and dip in beaten egg. Roll in bread crumbs. Fry until golden on both sides. Set aside. Soak dried mushrooms for at least an hr., then cook for 20-30 min. until tender. Strain and save bouillon. Wash, chop and salt cabbage. Put it in pot and pour over mushroom bouillon. Simmer briefly, then season with ground cloves. Sprinkle with sugar and cinnamon. Chop onions and cooked mushrooms, and brown in butter. Combine with simmered cabage and mix everything well. Arrange fish fillets and cabbage in a casserole; cover with sour cream. Bake in 350° oven for 30-40 min. until set. Drizzle with melted butter and garnish with chopped parsley. Serve with potatoes.

BREAM WITH APPLES AND HORSERADISH
ЛЯЩ З ЯБЛУКАМИ ТА ХРОНОМ

2½ lbs. bream, or similar fish
¼ c. vinegar
1 carrot
1 onion
1 parsley root
1 root of horseradish
½ lb. sour apples
1 bunch dill
salt to taste

Clean and scale bream. Cut off head, tail and fins. Slice into serving-sized portions. Sprinkle with salt. Place in pot with cold water with vinegar added. Let sit for 10 min. Drain. Pour 5 c. hot salted water over fish. Simmer on low heat for 30 min. Add cut up carrot, onion and parsley. Cook for 15 min. more. Serve shredded horseradish mixed with shredded sour apples as garnish. Serve with boiled potatoes sprinkled with chopped dill.

UKRAINIAN STUFFED PIKE
ФАРШОВАНА ЩУКА ПО-УКРАЇНСЬКОМУ

2 lbs. pike
1 carrot
1 beet
2 onions
2-3 bay leaves
1 lb. white bread
½ c. milk
2 egg yolks
1 T. farina
2 T. oil
1 lemon
salt, pepper, nutmeg to taste

Scrape off scales of fish. Remove fins and head and rinse pike. Cut away skin beginning around head and carefully moving towards tail, keeping skin in one piece. Set the skin aside. Clean and wash fish. Remove flesh from bones. Wash and cut up beet and carrot. Combine with peeled and chopped onion. Simmer a bouillon from pike head, bones and prepared vegetables for 60 min. Add bay leaves in the last few minutes. Strain bouillon and remove fish bones. Soak bread in milk and brown in same oil as onion. Combine with fish and grind mixture in meat grinder. Add egg yolks, milk and farina. Season with pepper, salt and nutmeg. Stir stuffing well and use to fill pike skin. Tie with string. Place in pot over vegetables. Pour over bouillon. Simmer on a very low heat (in order to prevent skin from bursting) about 50-60 min. Transfer stuffed fish to serving plate. Slice and decorate with lemon, sprinkle with dill or parsley. Serve with horseradish sauce.

ROLL-UPS FROM PIKE
ЩУЧІ КРУЧЕНИКИ

3 lbs. pike
6 T. flour
3 T. butter
1 parsley root
1 carrot
3 bay leaves
4 peppercorns
pepper and salt to taste

For filling:
½ c. white bread
2 onions
3 fresh eggs
3 T. butter
pepper and salt to taste

Wash and clean pike. Cut off head, fins and tail. Remove bones. Slice filleted pike into rectangular pieces and lightly pound them. Place head and bones in pot with cold water and cook for 30-40 min. *For filling:* Grind scraps from fillets with bread soaked in water. Add finely cut and slightly browned onion. Combine with eggs and butter. Sprinkle with pepper and salt. Mix everything well. Place filling in the middle of each fillet. Roll up and tie with thread. Dredge with flour. Fry in butter until golden on both sides. Place fried fish rolls in pot. Pour over bouillon, made of head and bones. Slightly brown flour, then add to bouillon constantly stirring. Add cut roots of parsley and carrots. Sprinkle with pepper. Simmer on low heat for 30-40 min. Add bay leaf last three minutes. Arrange roll-ups on platter with vegetables and pan liquid. Accompany with boiled potatoes.

KIEV-STYLE ROLL-UPS FROM PIKE
ЩУЧІ ЗАВИВАНЦІ ПО-КИЇВСЬКІ

2 lbs. pike fillets
2 eggs, beaten
3 T. butter
¼ c. crumbs
salt to taste

For filling:
1 c. rice
2 c. milk
6 eggs, hard-boiled
2 T. butter
salt to taste

Wash and fillet pike without damaging skin. Place fish on wooden board with skin side down. Sprinkle with salt and slice into rectangular 2 x 4 inch pieces. Cook rice in milk, and mix with chopped boiled eggs and butter. Spread filling onto every piece of fish, and roll up tightly. Tie with string. Dip in beaten eggs. Dredge in crumbs and brown in butter. Transfer to casserole and bake covered in 350° oven for 30-35 min. Serve with green salad.

FISH "SAUSAGES" IN SAUCE
ЩУЧІ КОВБАСКИ З ПІДЛИВОЮ

1 lb. pike fillet
½ lb. salt pork
2 onions
1 tomato
1 T. bread crumbs
5 T. oil
1 c. sour cream sauce
salt & pepper to taste

Wash and cut fillet of pike. Combine with salt pork and 1 peeled and cut up onion. Grind mixture in meat grinder. Sprinkle with pepper and salt. Mix well. Form into little "sausages." Roll them in bread crumbs. Fry in very hot oil to deep brown. Place in pot. Pour over sour cream sauce, adding tomato and onion. Bake in 350° oven for 30 min. until done. Serve with fried potatoes. (See sour cream sauce in *Sauces and Gravies*)

FRIED SHAD WITH TOMATOES
СМАЖЕНИЙ З ТОМАТАМИ

1 lb. shad, or similar fish
2 T. flour
5 T. oil
1 lb. tomatoes
salt and pepper to taste

Clean, wash and slice filleted shad into small pieces. Sprinkle them with salt and pepper. Roll in flour and fry in deep oil in a skillet until golden on both sides. For garnish cut tomatoes in halves, sprinkle with salt and pepper and fry.

HALIBUT BAKED WITH POTATOES
ПАЛТУС ЗАПЕЧЕНИЙ З КАРТОПЛЕЮ

1 lb. halibut
1 onion
1 lb. potatoes, boiled
1 c. white sauce
1 T. bread crumbs
3 T. butter
1 bunch dill
salt and pepper to taste

For white sauce:
½ c. flour
1 T. butter
2 c. meat bouillon
1 onion
1 parsley root
1 celery stalk
1 T. butter
½ lemon
salt to your taste

Slice skined and boned fillet of halibut into small pieces, and place into a well-buttered casserole. Cover with finely chopped and slightly browned onion and arrange wedges of boiled potatoes on top. Pour over white sauce and sprinkle with bread crumbs then drizzle with melted butter. Bake in 350° oven for 40 min. Serve with finely chopped dill. *To prepare sauce*, use leftover meat bouillon. Warm white flour in skillet in butter, constantly stirring (do not let flour change its color). Add a small part of bouillon to slightly cooled flour, mix well until there are no lumps, and then gradually add the rest of bouillon, stirring continuously. Bring sauce to boil, add chopped onion, root of parsley and celery and simmer for 20 min. Season with lemon juice and add salt. Strain through sieve, pushing vegetables through with wooden spoon or spatula. Add butter.

CODFISH BAKED WITH POTATOES
ТРІСКА ЗАПЕЧЕННАЯ З КАРТОПЛЯМИ

1½ lbs. potatoes
1 lb. cod fish
1 c. sauce
1 c. bread crumbs
3 T. butter
pinch of parsley or dill
salt to taste

For white sauce:
½ c. flour
1 T. butter
2 c. meat bouillon
1 onion
1 parsley root
1 celery stalk
1 T. butter
½ lemon

Wash and boil potatoes. Slice cleaned, washed, skinned and boned fish into small pieces. Season them with salt and pepper. Transfer into well-greased casserole. Cover layer of fish with layer of wedges of boiled potatoes. Sprinkle with salt. Cover with sauce (See in *Sauces and Gravies*); top with bread crumbs. Drizzle melted butter. Bake in 350° oven for 30-35 min. Serve with finely chopped parsley or dill.

COOKED COD
ВАРЕНА ТРІСКА

1 lb. codfish
1 carrot
1 onion
1 stalk celery
1 bunch parsley
2 bay leaves
3 peppercorns
¼ t. salt
¾ c. tomato paste
2 lbs. potatoes

Slice cleaned and washed codfish into steaks. Salt them and place in refrigerator for 30 min. Wash and cut carrot, onion, celery, parsley, and place in pot. Add bay leaves, peppercorns, salt, and cover with water. Simmer for 10-15 min. Strain vegetable bouillon. Set it aside. Place fish steaks in stewing pot, and cover with hot vegetable liquid. Cook on a low heat for 30-40 min. Add tomato paste. Sprinkle with finely chopped parsley and serve with whole boiled potatoes.

COD COOKED IN MILK
ТРІСКА ВАРЕНА В МОЛОЦІ

1 lb. cod
2 c. milk
1 onion
1 bay leaf
3 peppercorns
2 lbs. potatoes
2 T. butter

Place steaks of cod fillet in pot. Sprinkle with salt. Pour over cold water. Bring to boil, then drain. Add fresh water and bring to boil for the second time, and drain. Add finely chopped onion, salt, pepper and bay leaf, and hot milk; simmer on low heat for 30-35 min. Serve with boiled potatoes.

COD AND FARMER CHEESE CUTLETS
РИБ'ЯЧІ КОТЛЕТКИ З ТРІСКИ ТА СЕЛЯНСЬКОГО СИРУ

1 lb. cod fillet
½ lb. white bread
1 onion
¾ lb. farmer cheese
2 T. oil
2 t. butter
salt to taste

Cut washed cod fillet and grind in meat grinder. Add white bread, soaked in water. Combine with chopped onion. Sprinkle with salt and grind for the second time. Grate farmer cheese. Mix prepared mass with grated farmer cheese, and form into cutlets. Roll them in flour and fry in oil until a golden color. Bake in 325° oven for 15-20 min. Pour over melted butter and serve with mashed potatoes.

COD WITH CABBAGE
ТРІСКА З КАПУСТОЮ

1 lb. cod
2 T. flour
4 T. butter
2 lbs. cabbage
1 onion
2 T. oil
1 c. red sauce
salt, pepper and sugar to taste

For sauce:
1 onion
1 carrot
1 parsley root
1 T. butter
4 T. tomato paste
1 T. flour
5 c. bouillon
1 T. sugar
¼ c. sherry
salt and pepper to taste

Slice cod into small pieces. Sprinkle with salt and pepper and roll in flour and fry in butter. Wash, chop and brown cabbage in butter. Place in pot. Add chopped onion. Sprinkle with sugar. Pour over with oil and red sauce. Sauté for 20-30 min. until done. Transfer half of stewed cabbage into a pot. Place pieces of fried fish on it. Cover with a thin layer of cabbage, then red sauce. Stew for 1 hr. *To prepare sauce:* brown thinly chopped onion, carrot and parsley roots in butter. Add tomato paste. Simmer for 3-5 min. Constantly stirring, add lightly browned flour. Pour over bouillon and simmer for 25 min. Strain sauce. Season with salt, sugar and pepper. Bring to boil and add butter and sherry. Serve fish with prepared sauce and boiled potatoes sprinkled with dill.

COD CUTLETS
ТРІСКОВІ ТОВЧЕНИКИ

1 lb. cod fillet
½ lb. white bread
1 onion
1 raw egg
2 T. bread crumbs
2 T. oil
2 T. butter
salt and pepper to taste
parsley

Cut up washed cod fillet. Mix with pieces of white bread and sautéed onion. Grind the mixture in meat grinder. Add egg, pepper and salt. Mix again. Form into patties and roll them in bread crumbs. Fry in oil on both sides to a golden brown. Transfer to 350° oven and bake covered up for 20-30 min. Sprinkle with finely chopped parsley and drizzle with melted butter before serving with mashed potatoes.

FRIED NAVAGA
СМАЖЕНА РИБА-КІЗЛИК

1 lb. navaga
2 T. flour
3 T. oil
2 T. butter
salt and pepper to taste

Cut fish along backbone and remove lower jaw. Starting with the head, take off skin and fins. Do not cut belly. Gut fish through its mouth. Leave caviar inside. Season with salt and pepper. Roll in flour. Fry in oil. Drizzle with melted butter and chopped dill and serve with fried potatoes.

DNIPRO-STYLE FISH CUTLETS
РИБ'ЯЧІ ТЕФТЕЛЬКИ ДНІПРЯНСЬКІ

2 lbs. fish
4 onions, chopped and fried
3 T. flour
2 T. butter
3 eggs, hard boiled
1 raw egg
2 T. bread crumbs
½ bunch dill
½ bunch parsley
salt and pepper to taste

Serve with:
12 potatoes, fried
4 carrots in cream sauce
5 tomatoes, cut into wedges

Wash, clean and fillet fish, then cut into serving size pieces. Remove skin and pound fish. Mix well fried onion with chopped boiled eggs. Sprinkle with salt and pepper and divide stuffing in centers of each piece of fish. Roll up and flatten in shape of cutlet. Dredge in flour. Brush with raw egg and dip in bread crumbs. Fry in hot fat. Serve with fried potatoes, creamed carrots and fresh tomatoes. Decorate with chopped dill and parsley.

FRIED FLOUNDER WITH MUSHROOMS AND GHERKINS
СМАЖЕНА КАМБАЛА З ГРИБАМИ И КВАШЕНИМИ ОГІРКАМИ

10 boiled potatoes
2 lbs. flounder
3 T. flour
2 T. butter
5 T. oil
¼ lb. champignons
4 gherkins
2 onions
salt and pepper to taste

Wash, peel and boil potatoes in salted water. Clean and wash flounder; take off skin and slice fish into small pieces. Sprinkle with salt and pepper. Dip in flour. Fry in butter until golden on both sides. Transfer to greased casserole and bake in 350° oven for 20-30 min. Fry finely cut champignons in oil, add thinly cut gherkins and sauté for 10 min. Brown chopped onion and transfer to serving dish. Put baked fish on top and arrange boiled potatoes arround them. Cover both with mushrooms and gherkins. Drizzle with melted butter and sprinkle with chopped parsley.

COOKED EEL
ВАРЕНИЙ В'ЮН

1 lb. eel
2 carrots
2 onions
1 bunch celery
1 parsley root
2 bay leaves
3 peppercorns
1/4 t. salt
1 lemon
1 bunch dill
lettuce leaves
2 lbs. potatoes

Clean and wash eel, then skin it. Sprinkle with salt. If it has odor, place in deep dish and cover with 1 c. of salted milk and 1 T. of vinegar. Set it aside for 15 min. Cut up carrots, onions, celery and parsley. Cook vegetables in water seasoned with spices of your choice and bay leaves for 15 min. Transfer eel to pot, and pour over the strained vegetable bouillon. Simmer on low heat for 30 min. Transfer fish to serving plate. Add pieces of lemon and carrots. Decorate with lettuce leaves. Serve eel with boiled potatoes sprinkled with chopped dill and other vegetables.

VEGETABLE DISHES

CORN WITH VEGETABLES
КУКУРУДЗА З ОВОЧАМИ

4 ears corn
½ c. soybeans
1 bunch celery
1 onion
2 carrots
2 potatoes
1 T. honey or brown sugar
½ t. strong bitter mustard (German style)
3 walnuts
¼ lb. pumpkin
1 apple
3 T. butter

Cook corn in 5 c. salted water for 20-25 min. In separate pot cook soybeans. Drain liquid and set it aside. Cut corn off ear and combine with cooked soybeans. Brown chopped celery, onion, carrots and potatoes in butter. Transfer to pot. Pour over 2 c. corn water with honey and mustard added. Steam covered for 20-30 min. Add chopped walnuts, cubed pumpkin (seeded), peeled and cubed apple, cooked corn and soybeans. Simmer for 10 more min.

CORN SALAD
КУКУРУДЗА З ОВОЧАМИ

4 ears corn
½ head small cauliflower
¼ lb. tomatoes
¼ lb. cucumbers
½ c. oil
4-5 black olives
salt and pepper to taste

Wash and cook corn. Cut off ear and set aside. Wash and cook cauliflower in salted water. Break apart and cut up large pieces. Wash and slice tomatoes and cucumbers. Combine all prepared vegetables. Sprinkle with salt and pepper. Season with oil and decorate with sliced olives.

POTATOES STEWED WITH PRUNES
ВАРЕНА КАРТОПЛЯ ЗІ СЛИВАМИ

2 lb. potatoes
1 onion
½ lb. prunes
1 T. butter
3 c. beef bouillon or water
1 T. green parsley
salt and pepper to taste

Cut peeled potatoes in cubes and place in saucepan. Cover with bouillon and stew for 15-20 min. Slightly brown chopped onion. Combine with pitted prunes. Add to potatoes. Sprinkle with salt. Stew another 10 min. When ready sprinkle with green parsley.

COLD BEET SOUP
ТАРАТУТА ХОЛОДНА

1 lb. beets
½ c. pickles
2 onions
¼ t. horseradish
3 T. oil
¾ c. pickle juice
¾ c. beet liquid

Wash and peel beets. Cut in circles. Cover with water in pot and cook for 20-30 min. until tender. Drain, saving liquid. Add pickles and chopped onions. Combine oil, beet liquid and pickle juice. Season with horseradish. Stir into beets and refrigerate for 24 hrs before serving.

BEETS, APPLES AND KIDNEY BEANS SALAD
САЛАТА ЗІ БУРЯКОВ, ЯБЛУКОВ ТА ХВАСОЛИ

½ lb. kidney beans
1 lb. beets
1 lb. apples
4 T. oil
4 T. vinegar
salt and papper to taste

Wash, soak in cold water for 3 hrs. then cook kidney beans for 60 min. Wash and cook beets for 30-40 min. Peel them. Wash and peel apples. Cut beets and apples into cubes. Combine with cooked kidney beans. Shake vinegar and oil together to combine and pour over beans. Sprinkle with salt and pepper and serve.

MASHED KIDNEY BEANS, POPPYSEEDS AND POTATOES
ТОВЧОНКА

½ c. poppyseeds
¼ lb. kidney beans
1 lb. potatoes
1/3 lb. scallions
1 bunch green parsley
2 T. butter
2 T. sugar
salt to taste

Soak separately poppyseeds and kidney beans for 10 hrs. in cold water. Cook beans for 2 hrs then puree. Make a puree of poppyseeds and mix the two. Cook and mash potatoes; add finely cut scallions and parsley. Season with melted butter, sugar and pepper and stir together. This is a good side dish for poultry.

POTATO ROULADE WITH SAUERKRAUT
ЛЕЖНІ КАРТОПЛЯНІ

1 lb. potatoes
4 eggs
1/3 c. flour
½ lb. sauerkraut
1 onion
¼ lb. salt pork
¼ t. gray pepper
1 c. sour cream
salt to taste

Wash and boil potatoes, then cool, peel and mash. Mix in fresh eggs. Place mixture on floured board and pat into rectangle. In pot simmer chopped sauerkraut for 15 min., and season with salt and pepper. Add chopped onion browned in salt pork. Drain sauerkraut filling and spread evenly on top of potatoes to within 1 inch of edges. Roll up potatoes and brush roulade with melted fat. Transfer to well greased baking pan. Bake in 350° oven for 30 min. Serve with sour cream.

POTATO BUNS WITH PLUMS
КНЬІДЛІ

1 lb. potatoes
½ c. flour
½ egg
¼ lb. plums
1 T. sugar
3 T. butter
salt and pepper to taste

Wash and peel potatoes, grate them and place in sieve to drain. Mix grated potatoes with flour. Add salt and knead well. Shape into balls with fresh pitted plum inside each, and cook in salted water for 20-30 min. Drizzle with melted butter and serve.

FARMER PEA BUNS
ХОМИ СЕЛЯНСЬКІ

1 lb. peas
3/4 c. hemp seed
2 T. lard
salt and parsley

Wash and cook peas. Drain liquid, combine cooked peas with stirred hemp seed. Season with salt and mix well. Shape into patties, place in a greased baking pan and bake in 350° oven for 15 min. Sprinkle with parsley before serving.

SHEPHERD'S PIE STUFFED WITH POTATOES AND MEAT
КАРТОПЛЯНА ЗАПІКАНКА ФАРШОВАНА З М'ЯСОМ

¼ lb. beef
2 lbs. potatoes
1 t. lard
3 eggs
1 onion, chopped
2 T. crumbs
pinch chopped dill
salt and pepper to taste

Wash and cut beef into small pieces. Transfer to pot, add water to cover, and stew for 30-45 min. Boil peeled potatoes. Grind them. Add salt, 2 eggs and mix well. Process meat through meat grinder. Add browned onion and season with salt and pepper. Grease and sprinkle baking pan with bread crumbs. Place half of potato mixture on it in an even rectangle or circle. Spread meat filling over it and cover with the rest of potato mixture. Smooth out and brush with whipped egg. Sprinkle with crumbs and bake in 350° oven for 30-40 min. Serve with melted butter. Sprinkle with chopped dill.

BOILED POTATOES WITH MUSHROOM FILLING
КАРТОПЛЯ ФАРШОВАНА ГРИБАМИ

2 lbs. potatoes
½ c. dried mushrooms
2 onions
3 T. butter
2 eggs
2 T. bread crumbs
1 bunch parsley
1 bunch dill
1 c. mushroom bouillon
salt and pepper to taste
sour cream

Boil large peeled potatoes until half done, and drain. Cook finely chopped mushrooms for 20 min. Mix them with browned chopped onion and chopped hard boiled eggs. Sprinkle with finely chopped parsley and dill. Add bread crumbs and salt and mix well. Cut out the center of each boiled potato, and fill with mushrooms. Place in pot. Add mushroom bouillon and simmer for 35-40 min. Put a dab of sour cream on each potato and sprinkle with chopped dill.

POTATO PATTIES KIEV-STYLE
КАРТОПЛЯНІ ТОВЧЕНИКИ ПО КИЇВСЬКОМУ

2 lbs. potatoes
2 T. butter
2 eggs
2 T. potato starch flour
½ c. water

For filling:
¼ c. dried mushrooms
5 T. flour
1 c. milk
1 egg
4 T. bread crumbs
1 bunch dill
salt to taste

Boil peeled potatoes, and mash. Add butter and fresh eggs, 2 T. flour dissolved in cold water and sprinkle with salt. Stir well. *For filling*: Wash and soak mushrooms in cold water for 60 min. Cook them in the same water for 30-40 min., then finely chop. In butter brown 3 T. flour and a sprinkle of salt. Constantly stirring, pour over scalded milk, and mix until sauce gets thick. Add chopped boiled mushrooms and stir well. Divide prepared potato mixture into portions. Place in the center of each portion a spoonful of milk sauce with mushrooms. Pat into an oval shape and roll in flour. Dip in beaten egg and roll in bread crumbs. Fry until golden on both sides. Serve with mushroom sauce sprinkled with chopped dill.

POTATO PATTIES WITH MUSHROOMS AND RICE
КАРТОПЛЯНІ ТОВЧЕНИКИ З ГРИБАМИ ТА РИСОМ

2 lbs. potatoes
1 egg
3 T. rice
1/3 c. dried mushrooms
½ T. onion, minced
2 T. lard
1 T. flour
2 T. butter
salt and pepper to taste

Peel, wash and boil potatoes. Mash them thoroughly. Stir in egg and season with salt and pepper. Mix well and make patties. Wash and cook rice. Soak dried mushrooms for 60 min. in cold water. Cook them in the same water for 30-40 min., then finely chop and slightly brown them in butter with chopped onion. Season with salt and pepper and stir well. Combine with cooked rice and mix well. In the middle of each potato patty, place prepared filling. Seal edges, roll in flour and then fry in hot lard until golden on both sides. Serve with melted butter.

POTATO PATTIES
КАРТОПЛЯНІ СІЧЕНИКИ

1 lb. potatoes, boiled
1 egg
1 T. flour
2 T. oil
2 T. melted butter or ½ c. sour cream
salt to taste

Mash boiled potatoes thoroughly. Add egg and mix well. Divide into portions, and shape into patties. Roll them in flour. Fry in hot oil until golden on both sides. Serve with melted butter or sour cream.

POTATO PANCAKES
КАРТОПЛЯНІКІ

1 lb. potatoes
1/3 c. flour
1 egg
¼ t. baking soda
1 t. sugar
1 T. lard
1/3 c. sour cream

Peel, wash and boil potatoes. Mash them thoroughly. Add flour, egg, soda, salt and sugar. Mix well. Fry spoonfuls of mixture in hot lard. Serve with sour cream.

SIMPLE POTATO PANCAKES
ДЕРУНИ ЗВИЧАЙНИ

2 lbs. potatoes
1/3 c. flour
4 T. oil
2 onions, chopped
½ c. sour cream

Grate peeled fresh potatoes. Add salt and flour. Mix well for uniform batter. Fry spoonfuls of mixture in hot oil until golden on both sides. Serve hot with browned onion and sour cream.

POTATO PANCAKES WITH EGGS
ДЕРУНИ З ЯЙЦЕМ

2 lbs. potatoes
2 eggs
2 T. bread crumbs
4 T. lard
salt & pepper to taste
½ c. mushrooms

Peel and wash potatoes. Grate them and place in sieve to drain. Add eggs. Stir thoroughly. Add bread crumbs, sprinkle with salt. Mix thoroughly. Fry spoonfuls of mixture in hot lard. Top with sour cream and serve hot. For garnish use fried mushrooms.

POTATO ROLL-UPS WITH PEAS
КАРТОПЛЯНІ ЗАВИВАНЦІ З ГОРОХОМ

2 lbs. potatoes
2 eggs
2 t. potato starch, or flour
1 c. dried peas
2 T. bread crumbs
1 onion
3 T. lard
4 T. sour cream
salt and pepper to taste

Peel, wash and cook potatoes. Drain and mash them thoroughly. Add eggs. Stir in potato starch or flour and salt. Mix to a smooth batter. Wash and soak dried peas in 3 c. water for 60 min. Cook in the same water until tender. Drain in colander. Process through meat grinder. Chop onion and brown in lard; combine with ground peas. Sprinkle with pepper and salt. Place potato mixture in rectangle on damp towel. Spread it evenly. Cover with filling. Roll up and seal edge. Transfer to greased baking pan. Brush with beaten eggs and sprinkle with bread crumbs, then bake in 350° oven for 30-40 min. Serve with melted butter or sour cream.

CABBAGE STUFFED WITH MEAT AND RICE
КАПУСТНІ СТРАВИ

1-1½ lb. head of cabbage
1 T. vinegar
3 T. butter
3 T. rice
1 onion
1 lb. beef, veal, pork or lamb, cooked
1 c. sour cream
salt and pepper to taste

Wash, drain and core cabbage. Place cabbage in pot of boiling salted water with vinegar added. Bring to boil. Cook for 10-15 min. until crisp tender. Drain water. Set aside cabbage to cool. Brown chopped onion in butter. Wash and cook rice. Grind meat in meat grinder. Combine with cooked rice and browned onion. Season with salt and pepper. Mix well. Carefully, without tearing leaves, place meat between leaves of cabbage. Press leaves together. Transfer stuffed cabbage to baking pan. Pour over melted butter. Cover and bake in 350° oven for 1 hr. Cut in serving portions. Pour over with stewed liquid and serve with sour cream.

CABBAGE WITH MILLET STUFFING
КАПУСТА ТУШКОВАНА ПШОНОМ

1-1½ lb. head of cabbage
3 T. millet
4 carrots
2 parsley roots
3 onions
3 T. lard
1 egg
½ c. liquid
1 c. sour cream
salt and pepper to taste

Wash, drain and cook cabbage as above. Set aside. Cook millet. Cut peeled and washed carrots and parsley roots in cubes. Chop onion, brown it and mix with cooked millet and vegetables. Add egg. Sprinkle with salt and pepper. Mix thoroughly. Lift leaves of cabbage and place stuffing between them. Press leaves together and place stuffed cabbage in baking pan. Pour over melted lard. Bake in 350° oven for 20-30 min., then when it gets a golden color, transfer to stewing pot and stew covered for 30 min. until ready. Cut in portions, pour over sour cream and sprinkle with green parsley.

STEWED SAUERKRAUT WITH MUSHROOMS
КВАШЕНА КАПУСТА ТУШКОВАНА ГРИБАМИ

1/3 c. dried mushrooms
2 lbs. sauerkraut
½ c. mushroom bouillon
1 onion, chopped
1 T. flour
½ c. sour cream
salt to taste

Wash and soak mushrooms for 1 hr. Cook in the same liquid for 30 min, then chop finely. Drain sauerkraut. Place in pot, pour over mushroom bouillon and stew for 15 min. Brown chopped onion in lard. Mix it with cooked mushrooms. Slightly brown mixture. Sprinkle with flour and fry 5 more min. Season with sour cream and mix well. Combine with sauerkraut and stew for 15-20 min.

BAKED CABBAGE
ПЕЧЕНА КАПУСТА

1-1½ lb. head of cabbage
1 onion
½ c. sour cream
1 T. flour
1 T. bread crumbs
½ c. melted butter
2 T. lard
salt and pepper to taste

Clean, wash and shred cabbage. Sprinkle with salt. Place in pan and stew 15-20 min. until set. Brown chopped onion in butter. Mix it with sour cream and flour. Combine with stewing cabbage. Sprinkle with salt, pepper and breadcrumbs. Stir well. Add melted lard. Bake in 350° oven for 30-40 min. Pour over additional sour cream before serving.

CABBAGE PUDDING
ПІННИК З КАПУСТИ

2 lb. head of cabbage
2 c. milk
1 onion
1 T. sugar
3 eggs
3 egg whites
3 T. butter
½ c. bread crumbs
salt and pepper to taste

Clean, wash, and shred cabbage. Place in a pot with 2 c. scalding milk. Simmer for 15-20 min. until set. Drain and process through meat grinder. In butter brown finely chopped onion. Mix 3 eggs with sugar. Combine them with cabbage and browned onion. Beat egg whites to a froth. Fold into cabbage mixture along with bread crumbs. Sprinkle with salt and pepper. Drizzle with melted butter. Transfer to covered casserole. Place in a larger pot, and pour in 1 to 2 inches boiling water. Cover and simmer for 30-40 min. Serve with boiled potatoes and sour cream. Mushroom sauce is also a good addition.

CABBAGE PATTIES WITH APPLES
СІЧЕНИКИ З КАПУСТИ ТА ЯБЛУК

2 lb. head of cabbage
½ c. farina
¼ lb. apples
1 egg
3 T. bread crumbs
3 T. lard
salt to taste

Wash, clean and dice cabbage. Place in pot. Pour over boiling water to cover. Add salt and cook for 15-20 min. until tender. Slightly brown farina in butter. Constantly stirring, add it to cabbage. Stew 20 more min. Wash, peel and dice apples. Slightly brown them in butter. Add to stewed cabbage along with egg. Sprinkle with salt and shape into patties. Roll them in bread crumbs. Fry until golden on both sides. Serve with boiled or mashed potatoes and sour cream.

CABBAGE STUFFED WITH RICE AND MUSHROOMS
ГОЛУБЦІ З РИСОМ ТА ГРИБАМИ

1-1 ½ lb. head of cabbage
¼ lb. rice
½ c. dried mushrooms
1 onion
2 T. lard
2 t. chopped parsley
5 T. melted butter
1 ½ c. sour cream
2-3 bay leaves
1 T. flour
salt and pepper to taste

Cook washed, cleaned and cored cabbage in salted water for 15-20 min. Drain and set water aside. Remove leaves of cabbage. Trim the thick part from the bottom of each leaf. Wash and cook rice until half done. Wash and soak dried mushrooms in cold water for 60 min. Cook them in the same water for 30 min., then chop finely. Mix with rice. Brown chopped onion in lard. Combine it with rice. Season with pepper, chopped parsley and salt. Mix well. Place mound of prepared filling in the middle of every cabbage leaf. Fold sides of leaf over filling and roll it up. Place cabbage rolls in pot seamside down. Pour over 1 c. sour cream and 2 c. of cabbage liquid. Stew in 350° oven for 40-50 min. Blend mushroom bouillon, ½ c. sour cream and flour. Bring it to boil. Add bay leaf, salt and pepper. Boil for 3-5 min. Add to stewed rolls during the last ten minutes. Sprinkle with chopped parsley and serve.

SALAD FROM SAUERKRAUT AND MUSHROOMS
САЛАТ З КВАШЕНОЇ КАПУСТИ ТА ГРИБІВ

1 lb. sauerkraut
1 onion
¼ lb. marinated mushrooms
pinch cloves
pinch cinnamon
2 T. sugar
2 T. oil

Mix sauerkraut with chopped onion. Cut up salted or marinated mushrooms. Season with cloves and cinnamon. Add sugar and drizzle with oil. Serve with finely chopped parsley.

SALAD FROM CABBAGE, CARROTS, PEPPER AND APPLES
САЛАТ З КАПУСТИ, МОРКВИ, ПЕРЦЮ І ЯБЛУК

1 lb. cabbage
2 carrots
¼ lb. pepper
½ lb. apples
1 c. lemon juice
½ t. salt
1 t. sugar
½ c. sour cream
3 T. chopped parsley

Clean, wash and cut cabbage into straws. Stir in salt. Drain and collect juice (it is very healthy drink). Mix cabbage with cut-up carrots, green pepper and peeled apples. Sprinkle with lemon juice. Add sugar and pour over sour cream. Sprinkle with chopped parsley and serve.

SALAD FROM CABBAGE, APPLES AND ONION
САЛАТ З КАПУСТИ, ЯБЛУК ТА ЦИБУЛІ

1 lb. cabbage
¼ lb. apples
1 onion
¼ c. vinegar
1 T. sugar
¾ c. sour cream
salt and pepper to taste

Clean, wash and cut cabbage into straws. Peel and cut apples, then sprinkle with vinegar so that they will not get dark. Add chopped onion. Pour over with sour cream mixed with sugar. Season with pepper and mix well.

SALAD FROM CAULIFLOWER
САЛАТ З ЦВІТНОЇ КАПУСТИ

2 lbs. cauliflower
2 T. oil
1 T. vinegar
1 T. sugar
1 egg, hard-boiled
3 scallions
salt and pepper to taste

Clean, wash and place cauliflower in water-vinegar bath for 10-15 min. Drain. Divide into florets. Rinse. Place in pot. Scald with hot salted water. Cook for 25-35 min., then cool. Season with oil mixed with vinegar, sugar and gray pepper. Add chopped boiled egg and finely chopped scallion and serve.

CAULIFLOWER SALAD ANOTHER WAY
САЛАТ З ЦВІТНОЇ КАПУСТИ ПО-ІНШОМУ

1 lb. cauliflower
1 lb. tomatoes
1 cucumber
½ lb. apples
½ c. sour cream
1 T. sugar
1 T. vinegar
2 T. chopped dill
salt and pepper

Wash and cook cauliflower in boiling salted water. Drain. Divide into florets. Add finely cut tomatoes, cucumbers and apples. Mix well and pour over sour cream with vinegar added. Sprinkle with sugar and salt. Season with chopped dill before serving.

CARROT SALAD WITH APPLES ANOTHER WAY
САЛАТ З МОРКВИ ТА ЯБЛУК ПО-ІНШОМУ

½ lb. carrots
¼ lb. apples
1 t. vinegar
4 T. sour cream
1 T. sugar
1 T. green parsley
salt to taste

Peel carrots and apples. Wash them and cut into straws. Mix together vinegar and sour cream with sugar and pour over. Sprinkle with salt and chopped parsley.

GRATED BEETS
ТЕРТІ БУРЯКИ

1½ lbs. beets
4 T. oil
2 onions
1 t. vinegar
½ t . cloves
salt and pepper to taste
3 T. sugar
1 sprig of parsley

Wash beets. Bake in 350° oven for 40-50 min. until ready, then peel. Process through meat grinder. Fry ground beets in oil. Brown chopped onion in oil and combine with beets. Add vinegar. Season with black pepper, sugar and ground cloves. Sprinkle with salt and sugar. Mix well. Serve with finely chopped parsley.

SALAD FROM BEETS AND MUSHROOMS
БУРЯКОВИЙ САЛАТ З ГРИБАМИ

1 lb. beets
½ c. dried mushrooms
2 red onions
½ c. oil
1 T. vinegar

Wash dried mushrooms, then soak them in cold water for 1 hr. Cook in the same water for 30 min., then finely chop. Wash and cook beets. Peel them. Cut into straws. Mix with chopped mushrooms. Cut onions into half slices. Combine everything. Season with oil and vinegar and serve.

BEETS STEWED IN SOUR CREAM
ВАРЕНІ БУРЯКИ ТУШКОВАНІ В СМЕТАНІ

1 lb. beets
1 onion
3 T. butter
1 c. sour cream

Wash beets. Bake them in 375° oven for 60-70 min. Peel and cut into straws. Add finely chopped browned onion. Fry beets with onion in butter for 7-10 min. Pour over with sour cream. Mix well. Stew for 15 more min.

BEETS STUFFED WITH RICE, APPLES AND FARMER CHEESE
БУРЯКИ ТУШКОВАНІ З РИСОМ, ЯБЛУКАМИ ТА СЕЛЯНСЬКИМ СИРОМ

1 lb. beets
1c. rice
2 apples
2 T. sugar
1/3 lb. farmer cheese
1 egg
2 T. butter
1 c. sour cream
salt to taste

Choose big beets of even size. Wash and cook them for 50-60 min. until tender. Drain. Peel beets and core. Cook rice, then drain. Wash, peel and grate apples. Combine them with sugar and grated farmer cheese. Mix well. Add egg and butter and mix thoroughly. Fill beets with prepared filling. Place in greased baking pan. Top with sour cream. Bake in 350° oven for 40 min. Serve with sour cream.

PANCAKES FROM BEETS AND FARMER CHEESE
БУРЯКОВІ МЛИНЦІ З СЕЛЯНСЬКИМ СИРОМ

1½ lb. beets
1 c. flour
1 lb. farmer cheese, grated
4 T. sugar
1 egg
1 c. milk
salt to taste

Wash beets. Cook them for 1 hr., and peel. Process through meat grinder and combine with flour. Stir farmer cheese with sugar and egg. Combine with beets. Pour over with milk. Sprinkle with salt. Mix well. Make pancakes and fry in butter. Serve with sour cream.

TOMATOES STUFFED WITH MUSHROOMS
ПОМИДОРИ ФАРШОВАНЫ ГРИБАМИ

1 lb. fresh mushrooms
3/4 c. sour cream sauce
2 lbs. tomatoes
4 T. butter
salt and pepper to taste

Finely chop fresh mushrooms. Brown in butter. Cover with sour cream. Mix well and warm up. Cut off top of washed tomatoes. Take out some pulp and fill cavities with prepared filling. Drizzle with melted butter and bake in 300° oven for 15 min.

STUFFED TOMATOES ANOTHER WAY
ФАРШОВАНІ ПОМИДОРИ ПО-ІНШОМУ

8-10 tomatoes
2 onions
1 T. butter
1/3 fillet of herring
2 eggs
2 T. mayonnaise
¼ c. grated cheese
salt and pepper to taste
parsley

Cut washed tomatoes in half. With spoon scoop out most of the pulp. Peel and chop onions, and brown in butter. Combine with fillet of herring and chopped hard boiled eggs. Process through meat grinder. Add mayonnaise, salt and gray pepper. Mix well. Fill tomato halves with prepared stuffing. Sprinkle with grated cheese and decorate with green parsley.

STUFFED ONION
ФАРШОВАНА ЦИБУЛЯ

1 lb. large, mildly flavored onions
¼ lb. cucumbers
½ lb. tomatoes
1 egg
½ c. mayonnaise
1 T. chopped green parsley
salt to taste

Peel large onions and remove inside, then chop up. Combine with diced tomatoes and peeled fresh cucumbers. Cook egg. Add chopped hard boiled egg to the filling. Sprinkle with finely chopped green parsley and combine with mayonnaise. Add salt. Mix filling and stuff prepared onions. Serve with mayonnaise.

EGGPLANT WITH MUSHROOMS AND ONIONS
СИНІ БАКЛАЖАНИ З ГРИБАМИ ТА ЦИБУЛЕЮ

1 lb. eggplans
½ lb. tomatoes
3 T. flour
2 T. butter
2 onions
¼ lb. fresh mushrooms
1/3 c. sour cream
1 T. chopped dill
2 T. grated cheese
salt and pepper to taste

Wash and cut eggplant and tomatoes in slices. Sprinkle with salt and black pepper. Roll in flour. Fry until golden on both sides. Brown finely chopped onion. Combine it with finely chopped mushrooms. Add salt and pepper. Mix well and fry for 10 min. until mushrooms are done. Pour over sour cream and bring to boil. Arrange eggplant and tomatoes on serving plate, and cover with mushrooms. Sprinkle with grated cheese and chopped dill. Serve with boiled new potatoes.

STUFFED EGGPLANT WITH MILLET
ФАРШОВАНІ БАКЛАЖАНИ З ПШОНОМ

2 lbs. eggplant
2 onions
1 c. dried mushrooms
½ c. millet
2 T. lard
1 egg
2 T. bread crumbs
2 T. butter
1 T. chopped dill
salt and pepper to taste

Wash eggplant and cut in halves. Remove center portions and finely chop, then brown in lard. Chop onions. Brown them in lard. Wash and soak dried mushrooms in cold water for 1 hr. Cook in the same water for 30-40 min., then finely chop. Cook millet in mushroom bouillon. Combine millet with browned onion, mushrooms and eggplant. Add egg, salt and pepper and mix well. Stuff eggplant with mixture. Place on well greased baking pan. Sprinkle with bread crumbs. Bake in 350° oven for 30-40 min. Serve with melted butter and finely chopped dill.

STUFFED PEPPERS
МЕЖИВО З ПЕРЦЮ

2 lbs. green peppers
½ lb. cabbage
½ lb. carrots
1 root of parsley
1 celery stalk
2 onions
2 T. oil
2 T. sugar
2 T. chopped parsley
¾ lbs. tomatoes
3 T. tomato paste
salt to taste

Wash peppers and core, then cook in boiling salted water for 3 min. Drain. Wash and finely cut cabbage, peeled carrots, parsley and celery. Stew in a pot for 20-30 min. Add sugar and salt. Mix with browned chopped onion. Sprinkle with chopped green parsley. Stuff prepared peppers with filling. Brown tomato paste and cook with tomatoes for sauce. Add sugar, salt and vinegar and serve with peppers.

PEPPERS STUFFED WITH FARMER CHEESE
ФАРШОВАНИЙ ПЕРЕЦЬ З СЕЛЯНСЬКИМ СИРОМ

2 lbs. red peppers
¾ lb. farmer cheese
2 eggs
2 T. sugar
1 T. flour

For gravy:
1 c. milk
1 egg
¾ lb. flour
salt to taste

Wash peppers, core and drain. Grate farmer cheese, and stir in eggs, sugar and salt. Stuff peppers with farmer cheese. Place in a stew pot. *For gravy:* beat milk with raw egg and flour. Sprinkle with salt and pour over stuffed peppers. Stew for 45 min. Serve with boiled new potatoes.

ASPARAGUS BAKED IN MILK
АСПЕРЖ ПЕЧЕНИЙ У МОЛОЦІ

2 lbs. asparagus
1 t. sugar
1 c. milk sauce
3 T. butter
2 T. bread crumbs
salt to taste

Wash asparagus, remove tough scales and bottom portions. Cut asparagus in 1-inch pieces and place in pot with hot water. Add sugar and cook for 15-20 min. Drain. Place in casserole and cover with milk sauce (see Sauces and Gravies). Sprinkle bread crumbs and drizzle with butter. Bake in 350° oven for 40 min.

SPINACH BABKA
БАБКА З ШПІНАТУ

1 lb. spinach
½ lb. bread
1 c. milk
2 eggs
4 T. butter
1 T. sugar
2 T. bread crumbs
salt to taste

Wash and remove stems from spinach. Place in pot and scald with 2 c. boiling water. Cook on medium heat for 10-15 min. Drain and puree. Stir well. Soak bread in milk. Add melted butter, egg yolks and sugar. Mix well. Combine with spinach. Sprinkle with salt and melted butter. Mix again. Combine mixture with whipped egg whites. Butter a casserole and sprinkle with bread crumbs. Pour in spinach and bake in 350° oven for 50 min. Serve with melted butter.

HALUSHKY-DUMPLINGS FROM POTATOES
ГАЛУШКИ КАРТОПЛЯНІ

½ lb. potatoes, boiled
1 fresh potato
1 egg
1 onion
2 T. flour
1 T. oil
1 pinch red pepper
1 pinch salt
sour cream

Wash potatoes. Peel 1 potato and grind in meatgrinder. Cook other unpeeled potatoes in salted water. Drain, cool, peel and grind them in meat grinder. Combine with ground fresh potato and mix with egg. Add finely chopped onion browned in oil. Combine with flour and stir. Season with salt and red pepper and mix. Cook spoonfuls of batter in simmering salted water at a slow boil for 8-10 min. Remove with slotted spoon to colander; transfer to serving plate and drizzle with butter. Serve with sour cream or melted butter. Can also be served with fried mushrooms to accompany meat dishes.

CAULIFLOWER FRIED IN BUTTER
ЦВІТНА КАПУСТА СМАЖЕНА У МАСЛІ

1 cauliflower
2 T. flour
4 T. butter
1 T. parsley
salt & pepper to taste

Clean and cut up cauliflower. Cook in salted water for 10-15 min. Roll in flour. Fry in butter. Drizzle with melted butter. Sprinkle with chopped parsley and serve.

CAULIFLOWER FRIED IN BREAD CRUMBS
ЦВІТНА КАПУСТА СМАЖЕНА У ХЛІБНИХ ОКРУШИНАХ

1 medium cauliflower
2 T. flour
2 eggs
2 T. bread crumbs
3 T. butter
salt and sugar to taste

Cut cleaned and washed cauliflower into quarters. Place in pot with salted water, and cook uncovered on high heat so that the color of cauliflower will not change. Drain the liquid and cut boiled cauliflower into slices ½ inch thick. Roll in flour and dip in beaten eggs, then in bread crumbs. Fry until golden on both sides.

CAULIFLOWER SOUFFLE
ВОЗДУШНИЙ ПИРІГ ЗІ ЦВІТНОЇ КАПУСТІ

½ c. farina
1½ c. milk
2 eggs
1 cauliflower
1 T. sugar
1 T. bread crumbs
3 T. butter
salt to taste

Cook farina in milk, constantly mixing. Clean and cut cauliflower in small pieces. Stew in milk for 15 min. Mix well and process through meat grinder. Add egg yolks mixed with sugar. Sprinkle with salt. Fold in whipped egg whites. Transfer to greased baking pan and sprinkle with bread crumbs. Drizzle with melted butter. Bake in 350° oven for 30 min. Cut before serving and drizzle with melted butter.

RED CABBAGE STEWED WITH KIDNEY BEANS
ЧЕРВОНА КАПУСТА ТУШКОВАНА З КВАСОЛЕЮ

1 c. kidney beans
2 lbs. red cabbage
3 T. butter
2 onions
½ T. flour
2 T. tomato paste
½ T. sugar
salt to taste

Wash kidney beans and soak for 2 hrs. Cook for 30 min. until tender. Wash and clean red cabbage. Cut into quarters and simmer in water and butter for 20-30 min. until tender. Combine drained cabbage, onions and cooked kidney beans. Add flour browned in butter, tomato paste, sugar and salt. Mix well and stew for 7-10 min. more. Serve with boiled potatoes or fried mushrooms.

RED CABBAGE STEWED WITH APPLES
ЧЕРВОНА КАПУСТА ТУШКОВАНА З ЯБЛУКАМИ

2 lbs. red cabbage
3 T. butter
1½ T. sugar
2 T. vinegar
3 apples
¾ c. sour cream
1 T. chopped parsley
salt to taste

Wash, clean and thinly cut red cabbage. Stew in pan in water and butter for 20 min. Add vinegar, sugar and salt, peeled and finely cut apples. Mix well. Stew for 15-20 min. more until ready. Season with sour cream and warm. Serve with finely chopped parsley.

PANCAKES FROM KOHLRABI
МЛИНЦІ З КОЛЬРАБІ

2 lb. kohlrabi
1 c. flour
2 eggs
1 T. sugar
½ t. baking soda
3 T. lard
½ c. sour cream
1 pinch salt

Wash and grate kohlrabi. Add flour, eggs, sugar, salt, soda and water. Stir well and fry spoonfuls in hot lard. Serve with sour cream.

KOHLRABI STUFFED WITH RICE AND MEAT
КОЛЬРАБІ З РИСОМ ТА М'ЯСОМ

2 lbs. kohlrabi
½ lb. meat, cooked
½ c. rice
1 onion
1 egg
2 T. lard
½ c. sour cream
½ c. tomato sauce
salt and pepper to taste

Wash and peel kohlrabi. Remove leaves and hollow out core. Cook kohrabi in salted water for 20-30 min. until half tender. Stir together chopped cooked meat, cooked rice and browned onion. Add egg, pepper and salt. Stuff kohlrabi with mixture. Place in a greased pot. Pour over sour cream and tomato sauce and simmer for 30 min. until ready.

CARROT BABKA
БАБКА З МОРКВИ

2 lbs. carrots
1 c. bread crumbs
3 T. butter
½ c. sour cream
3 eggs
2 T. sugar
2 T. flour
½ c. milk sauce or sour cream
salt to taste

Grate washed and peeled carrots. Mix with bread crumbs and slightly brown in butter. Stir together sour cream, egg yolks combined with sugar, 2 T. butter, flour and salt. Combine with whipped egg whites and mix thoroughly. Place mixture in a greased baking pan and bake in a 350° oven for 45-50 min. Serve with sour cream or milk sauce.

PENNYK FROM CARROT
ПІННИК З МОРКВИ

2 lbs. carrots
1 c. milk
2 T. butter
1 c. bread crumbs
2 eggs
2 T. sugar
¾ c. sour cream or whipped cream
salt to taste

Finely cut up washed and peeled carrots. Place in a pot. Pour over half of the milk and butter. Stew until done and mix with bread crumbs soaked in warm milk. Process mixture. Combine with egg whites stirred with sugar. Add whipped egg yolks and sprinkle with salt. Place in a 350° oven and bake in buttered casserole for 45-55 min. Serve with sour cream or whipped cream.

CARROT SICHENYKY
СІЧЕНИКИ З МОРКВИ

2 lbs. carrots
½ c. milk
3 T. butter
3 T. farina
1 egg
3 T. bread crumbs
½ c. sour cream
salt to taste

Cut washed and peeled carrots into thin slices. Stew with milk and butter for 20 min. Slightly brown farina in butter and mix well with stewed carrots. Stew for 15 min. more until ready. Set aside to cool. Process through meat grinder. Add fresh egg and sprinkle with salt. Divide mass into portions and make patties. Roll them in bread crumbs and fry in butter until golden on both sides. Serve with sour cream.

CARROT-FARMER CHEESE MEATBALLS
ТІФТЕЛЬКИ СЕЛЯНСЬКІ З МОРКВИ ТА СІРУ

2 lbs. carrots
½ c. milk
3 T. butter
5 T. farina
3 T. sugar
1 egg
½ lb. farmer cheese
5 T. bread crumbs
½ c. sour cream
salt to taste

Finely chop up washed and peeled carrots. Stew them with milk for 20 min. Add browned farina and sprinkle with sugar and salt. Mix well and stew 15 min. more until ready. Set aside to cool. Mix with fresh egg. Add farmer cheese and mix once again. Process through meat grinder. Form small rolls. Coat with bread crumbs and fry until golden. Serve with sour cream.

BAKED CARROTS WITH FARMER CHEESE
ПЕЧЕНА МОРКВА З СЕЛЯНСЬКИМ СИРОМ

2 lbs. carrots
½ c. milk
2 T. butter
4 T. farina
½ lb. farmer cheese
3 T. sugar
2 eggs
1 T. bread crumbs
½ c. sour cream
salt to taste

Finely chop up washed and peeled carrots. Process them through meat grinder. Stew with milk and butter for 20 min. Add browned farina and mix well. Stew for 15 min. more. Transfer half the stewed carrot to greased baking pan. Thoroughly combine farmer cheese with sugar and fresh eggs and place mixture above the layer of carrots. Cover with rest of the stewed carrot. Sprinkle with bread crumbs and bake in a 350° oven for 40 min. Serve with sour cream.

CARROT PANCAKES
МЛИНЦІ З МОРКВИ

2 lbs carrots
5 T. butter
1 c. flour
2 eggs
2 T. sugar
1 c. sour cream
salt to taste

Cut washed and peeled carrots. Brown them with butter and a little water. Set aside to cool. Process through meat grinder. Stir in flour, eggs, salt and sugar. Form mixture into pancakes and fry in butter. Serve with sour cream.

SAUCES & STOCKS

WHITE MEAT BOUILLON
М'ЯСНА ПІДЛИВА СВІТЛА

1 lb. meat bones
1 carrot
1 parsley
1 onion
5 c. water
salt to taste

Crush meat bones (of either beef, veal, pork, turkey, chicken or rabbit) into small 2-3 inch thick pieces. Wash them and place in pot. Pour cold water over bones. Bring to boil and simmer covered for 8 hrs. on low heat, periodically skimming. Bouillon from turkey, chicken or rabbit bones needs only 3 hrs. Add thinly sliced onion, cut up carrot and parsley 30 min. before bouillon is ready. Strain and use as base for a variety of sauces.

BROWN MEAT BOUILLON
М'ЯСНА ПІДЛИВА ТЕМНА

1 lb. meat bones
1 carrot
1 sprig parsley
1 onion
5 c. water
salt to taste

Crush meat bones (of either beef, veal, pork or chicken) into small 2-3 inch thick pieces. Wash them and brown with sliced onion, cut up carrot and parsley. Pour hot water over bones and simmer for 7 hrs. on low heat, periodically skimming. Strain bouillon and use as a base for a variety of sauces.

HOT TOMATO SAUCE
ГОСТРА ТОМАТНА ПІДЛИВА

1 onion
1 parsley sprig
1 carrot
2 T. fat
½ c. tomato paste
2 T. flour
1 c. white bouillon
2 T. butter
salt to taste

Finely chop onion, parsley and carrots. Brown them in hot fat. Add tomato paste. Simmer covered for 15 min. Add flour, mix everything well. Dissolve with white bouillon (see above). Add salt. Stew for 20 min. Strain mixture. Season with butter. Good for fried, stewed and cooked meat as well as for vegetable dishes.

BASIC WHITE SAUCE
ПРОСТА БІЛА ПІДЛИВА

1 qt. bouillon
2 T. butter
2 T. flour
1 parsley
1 onion
½ lemon
salt to taste

Warm flour in melted butter constantly stirring and not letting it brown. Cool and add 1 c. of hot bouillon. Mix well to get rid of lumps and add rest of the bouillon, little by little, mixing well each time. Bring sauce to boil. Add cut up onion and parsley and simmer for 30 min. Season with lemon juice and salt. Strain and add butter.

BASIC WHITE FISH SAUCE
ПРОСТА БІЛА ПІДЛИВА РИБ'ЯЧА

1 qt. fish bouillon
2 T. butter
2 T. flour
1 sprig parsley
1 onion
½ lemon
salt to taste

White fish sauce is made of fish bouillon the same way as white meat sauce.

MILK SAUCE
МОЛОЧНА ПІДЛИВА

5 c. milk
6 T. flour
3 T. butter
1 t. sugar
salt to taste

Slightly brown flour in butter. Slowly add hot milk, stirring to prevent lumps. Add sugar. Simmer 10 min. on low heat. Sprinkle with salt and strain. Good for vegetables and some meat dishes.

SOUR CREAM SAUCE
ПІДСМЕТАННИЧКА

2 T. butter
2 T. flour
2 c. sour cream
salt and pepper to taste

Slightly brown flour in butter. Mix with sour cream. Season with salt and pepper. Briefly simmer constantly stirring for 3-5 min. on low heat. Can be used with different flavorings (onion, parsley, celery, tomato, mustard or horseradish).

SOUR CREAM-TOMATO SAUCE
ПІДСМЕТАННИЧКА З ТОМАТОМ

Add 2 T. tomato paste to sour cream sauce. Good for meat, fish and vegetable dishes.

SOUR CREAM SAUCE WITH HORSERADISH
СМЕТАННА ПІДЛИВА З ХРІНОМ

1 T. flour
2 c. sour cream
1 horseradish root
1 t. butter
1 t. vinegar
1 pinch pepper
1 t. sugar
salt to taste

Brown flour without butter. Set aside for 5-10 min., then constantly stirring add to simmering sour cream. Mix well. Add salt and simmer about 5 min. Grate cleaned and washed horseradish. Warm in skillet in butter in order to get rid of sharpness. Season with vinegar, pepper and sugar. Simmer for 5 min. more, then mix with hot sour cream sauce. Cover and let stand for a few minutes for flavors to blend. Good for boiled meat, tongue, cold cuts or poached fish.

SOUR CREAM-TOMATO-ONION SAUCE
СМЕТАННА ПІДЛИВА З ЦИБУЛЕЮ ТА ТОМАТАМИ

2 onions
2 T. butter
1½ c. sour cream sauce
3 T. tomato paste
½ lemon
salt, pepper and sugar to taste

Mix finely chopped browned onion with sour cream sauce (see above). Gently heat 5-7 min., gradually adding tomato paste. Season with salt, pepper, sugar and lemon juice squeezed from fresh lemon. Bring to boil. This sauce is good for cutlets, meat balls and roasted meat.

WHITE ONION SAUCE
БІЛА ПІДЛУВА З ЦИБУЛЕЮ

2 onions
1 T. butter
1 T. vinegar
3 peppercorns
1/3 t. sugar
1 bay leaf
salt to taste

Finely cut up onion. Brown in butter on low heat until golden color. Add vinegar, peppercorns and bay leaf. Simmer covered for 5-7 min. Mix with red sauce (see above). Add salt and sugar. Simmer for 15 min. stirring continuously to prevent scorching. Season with butter. Good for fried and baked meat dishes.

MUSHROOM SAUCE
ГРИБНА ПІДЛИВА

10 dried mushrooms
1 T. fat
1 onion
1 T. flour
2 c. mushroom bouillon
1 T. butter
salt to taste

Wash dried mushrooms well. Soak them in cold water for 2-3 hrs. Cook until tender. Rinse well. Chop up finely. Fry in fat and return to bouillon. Finely chop onion. Brown it. Add flour and salt. Pour into mushroom bouillon. Mix well. Cook and season with butter. This sauce is good for potatoes, halushky and grits.

MAYONNAISE SAUCE
ПІДЛИВА-МАЙОНЕЗ

3 egg yolks
2 T. sugar
1 t. mustard
1 pinch of salt
1 pinch of pepper
1½ c. oil
2 T. vinegar

Stir fresh egg yolks with salt, pepper, sugar and mustard. Beat in oil. Add vinegar when mixture becomes thick. Mix well. This sauce is good for cold appetizers of meat and fish, and might be used as dressing on salads.

FLOUR DISHES

GRAIN DISHES AND KASHAS

CORN KISIEL
КУКУРУДЗЯНА КУЛЕША

¼ lb. corn flour
2 qts. water
1 c. milk (or ¼ c. sour cream, or 1/3 c. oil)

Constantly stirring, gradually pour corn flour into a pot of boiling water. Reduce heat. Add salt and mix well until ready (7-10 min.). Serve kisiel either with hot milk or with sour cream.

MAMALYGA
МАМАЛИГА

½ lb. corn flour
2 qts. water
1 c. milk or 2 t. butter
salt to taste

Brown corn flour in butter (do not let it change color). Transfer to pot and scald with boiling water. Keep stirring for 7-10 min. Serve with hot milk or seasoned with butter.

BUCKWHEAT LOAF
ГРЕЧАНИКИ

¾ c. milk
1 t. yeast
2 T. sugar
¼ stick butter
1 egg
1 lb. buckwheat flour
¼ c. oil
¾ c. sour cream
salt to taste

In bowl, stir yeast into warm milk and add sugar and salt. Pour in melted butter and fresh egg and mix. Gradually pour in sifted buckwheat flour, mix well and leave dough in a warm place for 15 min. until it rises. Knead again and leave in warm place for another 30 min. Transfer dough to floured board, roll it up into long thin loaves and brush tops with oil. Place them on a well-buttered baking pan. Set aside for 15-20 min. until they rise. Cut each loaf into small 1-1½-inch slices. Bake covered with foil in 350° oven for 45 min. Brush tops with slightly browned oil and serve with sour cream.

BUCKWHEAT PATTIES (GRECHANIK) IN CABBAGE LEAVES
ГРЕЧАНИКИ З КАПУСТЯНИМ ЛИСТЯМ

¾ c. milk
1 t. yeast
2 T. sugar
¼ stick butter
1 egg
1 lb. buckwheat flour
2 ½ lbs. cabbage
¾ c. sesame seeds
½ t. salt
¾ c. sour cream

In a pot, stir yeast in warm milk and add sugar and salt, then melted butter and egg. Gradually add sifted buckwheat flour and mix well. Leave dough in warm place for 30 min. until it rises. Knead well and leave in warm place for another 30 min. Cut dough into pieces and flatten into round buns. Place on cabbage leaves and bake in 350° oven for 15 min. Sprinkle half-ready "grechanik" with salted and moistened sesame seeds. Bake 30 min. more. Serve hot with sour cream.

BUCKWHEAT WITH SALT PORK
ЛЕМІШ З САЛОМ

1 lb. buckwheat flour
1 c. water
¼ lb. salt pork
salt to taste

Brown buckwheat flour in 325° oven for 5-7 min. Place it in enameled pot and scald with salted boiling water. Stir thoroughly and combine with small thin slices of browned salt pork and a little salt. Mix well and transfer to baking pan. Bake covered tightly with foil in 350° oven for 45 min. Serve as a side dish for beef steaks, poultry and mushroom dishes.

BUNS & PRETZELS

SWEET BUNS
ПАМПУШКИ

1/3 c. butter
2 c. water
¼ c. sugar
¼ lb. flour
3 eggs
¼ c. lard
¼ c. preserves
2 t. vanilla sugar

Place butter and sugar into boiling water. Gradually pour over flour constantly stirring so that no lumps form. Let it cool. Then add egg yolks and whipped egg whites while stirring. Fry a spoonful of the batter in hot lard until golden on both sides. Sprinkle with vanilla sugar and serve with jam or preserves.

BUNS WITH MARMALADE
ПАМПУШКИ З ПОВИДЛОМ

1 stick butter
2 c. water
5 T. sugar
½ lb. flour
4 eggs
1 c. preserves
¼ c. lard
2 t. vanilla sugar

Place butter and sugar into pot with boiling water. Gradually pour over flour and mix well for 3-5 min. in order to get smooth batter. Let it cool and stir. Add eggs and mix again. Let batter sit for 30 min. until it becomes thick. Place a few spoonfuls of the dough on floured board, make an indentation in the center of each and fill with preserves. Set aside for another 10 min. Fry in hot lard until golden. Sprinkle with vanilla sugar.

BUCKWHEAT BUNS (PAMPUSHKAS) WITH GARLIC
ГРЕЧАНІ ПАМПУШКИ З ЧАСНИКОМ

½ t. yeast
1 c. water
2 T. sugar
¼ t. salt
1 lb. buckwheat flour
3 T. butter
¾ c. oil
2 cloves garlic
salt to taste

Dissolve yeast in warm water and add sugar and salt. Gradually pour in buckwheat flour, mix well and set aside for 2 hrs. in warm place until it rises. Cut dough into circular shapes and flatten into small buns. Cook in boiling salted water for 10 min. Transfer to serving plate with melted butter. Combine crushed garlic and salt. Dissolve with oil and season hot *pampuskas*. Serve with hot borsch.

WHEAT BUNS WITH GARLIC
БІЛІ ПАМПУШКИ З ЧАСНИКОМ

½ t. yeast
1 c. water
2 T. sugar
¼ t. salt
1 lb. wheat flour
1 c. oil
2 cloves garlic

Dissolve yeast in warm water. Add sugar and salt and stir. Gradually pour in ¼ of flour. Mix well and leave dough for 1 hr. in warm place until it rises. Pour in remaining flour, mix and add 3/4 c. oil. Knead dough well and put aside for 30 min. Cut it into circular shapes and flatten them into small buns. Leave for 15 min. in warm place to raise. Transfer to baking pan and bake in 350° oven for 30 min. Grate garlic, sprinkle with salt, dissolve in the rest of oil and a little of boiled water and season hot *pampuskas*. Serve with bouillon, beef and fish soups and hot borshch.

POTATO-CHEESE BUNS
СИРНІ МНИШКИ

4 medium potatoes
¼ lb. farmer cheese
1 c. milk
2 eggs
½ lb. flour
½ c. sour cream
1 bunch scallions
salt to taste

Wash, peel and boil potatoes. Drain them and cool. Process farmer cheese and boiled potatoes through meat grinder. Pour milk over the ground mixture. Add eggs. Sprinkle with salt and mix with flour. Knead well and roll into balls. Brown them in butter. Serve with sour cream and a scallion salad on the side.

PACKETS
СУПРОСЯВКИ

½ t. baking soda
½ c. milk
2 eggs
½ lb. flour
½ stick butter
¼ c. honey
salt to taste

Mix baking soda, milk and eggs in bowl. Add flour, mix well and knead. Transfer to wooden board and roll dough out thinly. Cut it into small rectangles and connect opposite corners. Drop them into salted boiling water but do not crowd them in pot. Cook for 15 min. After they rise, remove them with slotted spoon and brown in butter. Serve with honey.

PRETZELS (VERGUNY)
ВЕРГУНИ

3 c. flour
½ stick butter
¼ t. baking soda
1 egg
½ c. sour cream
1 T. vinegar
¼ c. vodka (horilka)
¼ t. salt
3 T. sugar
½ c. oil
4 T. powdered sugar
¼ t. vanilla

Combine flour, butter and baking soda and cut with 2 knives. Make a depression and pour in egg, sour cream, vinegar and vodka. Mix and add salt and sugar. Knead well. Roll dough out thinly. Cut in 1½ inch x 6 inch strips. Make 1½ inch cut in the middle of each strip, and pull through one end. Transfer to generously oiled pan. Fry until brown on both sides. Set aside. Sprinkle with powdered sugar and vanilla before serving.

SIMPLE PRETZELS
ПРОСТІ ВЕРГУНИ

3 egg yolks
3 T. sugar
¾ c. sour cream
¼ c. vodka (horilka)
1 lb. flour
1 c. salt pork
2 T. powdered sugar
1 T. vanilla
salt to taste

Stir sugar with egg yolks. Sprinkle with salt and combine with sour cream and horilka in bowl. Mix well. Gradually stir in flour and mix. Knead dough until it is smooth. Roll it out on wooden board as thinly as possible. Cut into strips, about 2 inches wide and 6 inches long. In the middle of each strip make a slit about 1½ inches long. Pull one end of each strip through the slit. Fry "verguny" in salt pork fat for 3-5 min. until they turn a golden color on both sides. Let them cool. Sprinkle with powdered sugar and vanilla before serving.

KIEV-STYLE PRETZELS
КИЇВСЬКІ ВЕРГУНИ

3 eggs
5 T. sugar
½ c. melted butter
2 T. cognac
¾ c. milk
¾ c. grated almond
1 lb. flour
¾ c. lard
salt to taste

Whip eggs with sugar and add melted butter, cognac and milk. Mix well. Add salt and grated almonds. Gradually stir in flour, and mix thoroughly. Knead dough well. Roll it out thinly and cut into strips 2 inches wide and 6 inches long. In the middle of each strip make a 1½-inch thick slit, and pull one end of strip through it. Fry "verguny" in lard for 3-5 min. until they turn a golden color on both sides. Let them cool. Sprinkle with powdered sugar and vanilla before serving.

VOLYN-STYLE PRETZELS
ВОЛИНСЬКІ ВЕРГУНИ

4 T. sugar
5 egg yolks
¼ c. oil
¾ lb. flour
¾ c. lard
1 pinch salt

Stir sugar with oil and egg yolks. Sprinkle mixture with salt. Gradually add flour and knead dough for 30 min. Roll it out thinly and cut into strips 2 inches wide and 6 inches long. In the middle of each strip make a 1½-inch slit, and pull one end of strip through it. Fry "verguny" in salt pork fat for 3-5 min. until they turn a golden color on both sides. Serve with tea, milk, coffee, or hot chocolate.

LVIV-STYLE PRETZELS
ЛЬВІВСЬКІ ВЕРГУНИ

4 T. sugar
5 egg yolks
¼ lb. butter
2 T. rum
1 t. vinegar
1 lb. flour
¾ c. lard
1 pinch salt

Stir sugar, egg yolks and butter. Add rum and vinegar and mix well. Gradually stir in flour. Sprinkle with salt. Knead well. Roll dough out thinly and cut into strips 2 inches wide and 6 inches long each. In the middle of each strip make a slit 1½ inches long. Pull one end of strip through the slit. Fry "verguny" in salt pork fat for 3-5 min. until they turn golden on both sides. Let them cool and sprinkle with powdered sugar. Serve with warm honey.

KONOTOP-STYLE PRETZELS
КОНОТОПСЬКІ ВЕРГУНИ

4 T. sugar
2 egg yolks
¾ c. milk
½ lemon
¾ lb. flour
juice of ½ lemon
¾ c. lard
1 pinch salt

Stir sugar with egg yolks. Pour over milk. Add grated lemon peel and lemon juice, sprinkle with salt and mix well. Gradually stir in flour and knead dough. Cover with towel and let sit for 10-15 min. Then roll dough out thinly and cut into strips 2 inches wide and 6 inches long. Make a slit about 1½ inch long in the middle of each strip and pull one end of strip through the slit. Fry *verguny* in lard for 3-5 min. until golden on both sides. Serve with cold milk.

SUBOTIN-STYLE PRETZELS
СУБОТИНСЬКІ ВЕРГУНИ

1½ lbs. flour
¼ c. sour cream
¼ c. vodka (horilka)
7 egg yolks
¼ lb. sugar
3 eggs
1 c. lard
2 T. powdered sugar
1 T. vanilla

Spread flour over wooden board and make a deep hollow in it. Pour in sour cream and horilka. Add egg yolks stirred with sugar, then eggs and mix everything with flour thoroughly. Knead dough well. Roll it out as thinly as possible and cut into strips 2 inches wide and 6 inches long. In the middle of each strip make a slit 1½ inches long and pull one end of strip through the slit. Fry *verguny* in lard for 3-5 min. until they turn golden on both sides. Serve with coffee, milk, hot chocolate or tea.

BABKAS, CAKES AND PIES

EGG BABKA
ЯЕЧНА БАБКА

6 eggs
1 stick butter
½ c. flour
2 c. cream
salt to taste

Stir eggs with butter. Constantly stirring, add flour. Sprinkle with salt. Add cream. Transfer to greased pan. Bake in 350° oven for 30 min. until it rises.

CHERRY BABKA
ВИШНЕВА БАБКА

1 lb. cherries
¼ lb. sugar
5 eggs
2/3 c. sour cream
¼ lb. flour
¼ t. cinnamon
2 T. bread crumbs
salt to taste

Wash and pit cherries. Place them in pot and add a cup of sugar. Stir in sugar with egg yolks and sour cream. Gradually add flour and mix well. Fold in whipped egg whites. Add cinnamon. Grease baking pan and sprinkle with bread crumbs. Transfer dough to pan and bake in 325° oven for 60 min.

APPLE BABKA
БАБКА ЯБЛОЧНА

1½ lbs. apples
4 eggs
½ c. sugar
½ c. sour cream
¼ stick butter
½ c. flour
2 T. cinnamon
salt to taste

Wash and peel apples. Grate half of the apples. Cut rest into wedges. Stir sugar with egg yolks. and sour cream. Constantly stirring, add flour. Sprinkle with cinnamon. Add grated and cut up apples. Mix everything. Fold in whipped egg whites. Transfer batter to buttered baking dish. Bake in 325° oven for 30 min.

FRUIT CAKE
ПОВИДЛЯНКА

5 eggs
½ c. sugar
3 c. jam
¼ c. rum or vodka
½ lb. farina
2 T. butter
¼ lb. grated nuts

Stir half the sugar with the egg yolks. Add stirred jam and vodka. Gradually fold in farina and whipped egg whites. Mix everything well. Place in a greased baking pan and sprinkle with remaining sugar and grated nuts. Bake in 350° oven for 35-40 min.

POUND CAKE
ПАПУШНИК

2 lbs. flour
½ qt. milk
6 eggs
1 stick butter
½ lb. sugar
¼ t. vanilla
1/3 c. powdered sugar
salt to taste

Scald half the amount of flour with scalding milk and stir thoroughly until smooth. Let cool. Cream sugar with eggs and stir into dough. Add the rest of flour and knead well. Srir in melted butter, sugar and vanilla. Fill greased baking pan with dough (½ its height in proportion) and put in a warm place. When dough doubles, place it in 350° oven for 50-60 min. Dust with powdered sugar before serving.

SOUR CREAM CAKE
СМЕТАННИК

5 egg yolks
¼ stick butter, melted
½ c. sour cream
½ c. sugar
½ c. flour
1 T grated lemon peel
salt to taste

Stir egg yolks, butter, sour cream and sugar. Gradually add flour. Sprinkle with salt. Add dried lemon peel and beat well. Place dough in greased and floured baking pan and bake in 325° oven for 45-50 min.

CHOCOLATE CAKE
ШОКОЛАДНИЙ ПИРІГ

4 eggs
¼ c. sugar
1½ stick butter
¼ c. melted chocolate
¼ lb. flour
1 c. raspberry jam
1 c. grated chocolate
1 c. grated walnuts
1 pinch of salt

Stir sugar with egg yolks. Mix with whipped butter and melted chocolate. Sprinkle with salt and gradually stir in flour. Add whipped egg whites. Transfer to well greased and floured baking pan. Bake in 350° oven for 30-35 min. Before serving, brush with raspberry jam and sprinkle with grated chocolate and walnuts.

HOLIDAY CAKE
СВЯТКОВИЙ ПАПУШНИК

2 lbs. flour
½ qt. milk
2 oz. yeast
6 egg yolks
½ lb. sugar
¼ t. vanilla
1 stick butter
½ c. powdered sugar
salt to taste

Place half of flour in a pot, scald with hot milk and stir thoroughly. Let mixture cool, add yeast, mix well and set dough aside in a warm place for 30 min. Cream sugar with egg yolks, sprinkle with salt and vanilla and add to dough when it rises. Gradually stir in the rest of flour and knead dough until it does not stick to your fingers. Add melted butter and knead once more. Place batter in greased baking pan (1/3 full) and put in warm place for 2 hrs. When the amount doubles, bake in 350° oven for 50-60 min. Dust cooled *papushnik* with powdered sugar.

PIDILIAN CAKE
ПІДИЛЯНСЬКИЙ ПАПУШНИК

½ qt. light cream
2 lbs. flour
2 oz. yeast
6 eggs
1 stick butter
½ lb. sugar
¼ t. vanilla
1/3 c. powdered sugar

Heat the light cream and stir half into half the flour. Add melted butter. Allow it to cool. Stir in yeast dissolved in warm light cream. Add egg whites with vanilla and mix well. Set aside for 30-40 min. Stir in egg yolks with sugar. Gradually add the remaining flour, knead well and set aside for 2 hrs. Then knead well until dough is no longer sticky. Transfer dough to greased baking pan (half full). Cover with cloth and allow to rise in warm place until doubled. Bake in 325° oven for 50-60 min. Allow to cool in pan. Remove and dust with powdered sugar.

LAYER CAKE WITH BLINTZES AND APPLES
СОЛОЖЕНИКИ З ЯБЛУКАМИ

1 stick butter
½ c. sugar
½ c. cream
4 eggs
1 T. grated lemon peel
1 c. flour
½ lb. apples
1 T. powdered sugar
1 T. vanilla
½ stick butter
salt to taste

Cream sugar with butter. Add cream, egg yolks and mix well. Combine with grated lemon peel. Gradually add flour and knead dough well. Fry thin blintzes in hot butter. Cover with towel to keep them warm. Place peeled and finely cut apples in pan, sprinkle with powdered sugar and vanilla, add ½ stick of butter and stew for 10-15 min. until they become soft. Place 1 T. stewed apples in the middle of each blintz, roll them up and place in a greased baking dish in two layers, one on top of the other. Cover with egg whites whipped with sugar and bake in a 350° oven for 15-20 min.

CHERRY CAKE KIEV-STYLE
КИЇВСЬКИЙ ВИШНЕВИ ПИРІГ

½ c. almonds
½ stick butter
3 eggs
3 T. sugar
1 T. grated lemon rind
¾ c. bread crumbs
½ c. cherry preserves
1/8 t. cinnamon

Scald almonds with boiling water. Drain. Remove their skins and crush them well. Mix butter and egg whites. Stir in sugar with egg yolks. Add crushed almonds. Stir mixture until it is smooth. Add grated dry lemon rind. Crush bread crumbs. Combine all ingredients with cherry preserves. Season with cinnamon. Mix well. Transfer batter to well greased baking pan and bake in 350° oven for 25-30 min. Set aside for 10 min. Cut into pieces and serve.

HONEY CAKES WITH POPPY SEED
МЕДІВНИКИ-ШУЛИКИ С МАКОМ

½ c. poppy seed
½ c. honey
1 egg yolk
½ c. milk
½ stick butter
¼ t. baking soda
1 lb. flour

For syrup:
½ c. poppy seed
2 c. honey
½ c. warm water

Scald poppy seed (amount needed for both buns and syrup) with boiling water. Drain, then scald with hot water for the second time. Set aside for 15 min. Drain. Combine ½ poppy seeds with ¼ c. honey. Stir rest of honey with egg yolk, then with honey and poppy seed. Add milk, butter, baking soda. Mix well. Constantly mixing, gradually pour in flour. Knead dough well. Roll it out 2 inches thick. Transfer to baking pan. Punch with fork. Bake in 350° oven for 30-40 min. Set aside to cool. Cut into small cakes. *For syrup:* constantly stirring, dissolve the rest of the poppy seed with warm boiled water. Add 2 c. honey. Serve cakes with poppy syrup in small pitcher.

DUMPLINGS (HALUSHKY)

UKRAINIAN HALUSHKY
УКРАЇНСЬКІ ГАЛУШКИ

2½ c. flour
¾ c. water
2 eggs
¼ c. butter or pig fat
⅓ c. sour cream

Sift flour. Make hollow in it and pour in water, 2 T. melted butter, salt and beaten eggs. Mix well. Knead dough. Roll it out ¼-inch thick. Cut into small pieces. Boil in salted water for 10 min. until they rise. Pour off water. Transfer *halushky* to a buttered pan and fry slightly. Salted pig fat cut in small pieces can be used instead of butter by those who want a real taste of Ukrainian *halushky*. Serve warm with sour cream.

RAISED HALUSHKY
ГАЛУШКИ

1 t. yeast
1 c. cream
3 eggs
½ stick butter
1½ lbs. flour
2 T. sugar
salt to taste

Combine egg whites with yeast dissolved in warm cream. Stir in half the flour and softened butter. Set aside for 30-40 min. When dough rises, pour in egg yolks stirred with sugar and mix well. Gradually add remaining flour and mix. Knead dough well and set aside for 1½-2 hrs. Then knead until dough ceases to be sticky. Transfer to wooden board and roll out into thin layer. Drop dough by spoonfuls into salted boiling water and cook covered for 5-7 min. Transfer to colander, rinse with hot water. Serve with browned salt pork nuggets.

BUTTER HALUSHKY
СОЛОДКІ ГАЛУШКИ

2 lbs. flour
¼ c. water
2 egg whites
½ stick butter
½ c. sour cream

Sift flour into bowl. Make an indentation in it and pour in warm water and egg whites whipped with salt. Add butter and work into thick dough with spoon (preferably wooden). Cover dough with towel and set aside for 20-30 min. Transfer to floured board and roll by hand into a long rope ½-inch thick. Cut into *halushky* and cook them in boiling salted water for 10-15 min. Transfer to colander, rinse with hot water, drain and slightly brown in butter. Serve with sour cream, ham or browned salt-pork cracklings. Warm in 325° oven for 3-5 min. before serving.

HALUSHKY WITH FARMER CHEESE
ГАЛУШКИ З СЕЛЯНСЬКОГО СИРУ

2 eggs
1 lb. farmer cheese
3 T. sugar
3 T. butter
1 c. flour
2 T. crumbs
salt to taste
½ c. sour cream

Grate farmer cheese and stir with eggs. Add sugar, melted butter. Sprinkle with salt and mix. Combine with flour and knead. Place on floured board. Cut in four equal pieces. Roll each piece into thin "sausage" and cut into small 2-inch pieces. Cook in salted boiling water for 7-10 min. until they rise to the surface. Roll in crumbs fried to a golden color. Place *halushky* on plate, pour over melted butter, and serve with sour cream.

HALUSHKY WITH FARMER CHEESE KIEV-STYLE
ГАЛУШКИ З СЕЛЯНСЬКОГО СИРУ ПО-КИЇВСЬКОМУ

1 lb. farmer cheese
¼ c. sugar
2 egg whites
¼ c. butter
1½ c. flour
salt to taste
½ c. sour cream

Grind farmer cheese in meat-grinder, sprinkle with salt and add sugar. Mix with whipped egg whites and butter. Gradually add flour and stir thoroughly. Roll dough tightly into ½-inch rope and cut into ½-inch pieces. Form these between floured hands into round *halushky* the size of large walnuts. Cook in salted water on low heat for 10-15 min. Serve with sour cream and melted butter and a green salad.

HALUSHKY FROM BUCKWHEAT
ГАЛУШКИ ГРЕЧАНІ

1½ c. buckwheat flour
3 c. water
1 egg
¼ lb. onion
3 T. salt pork fat
salt to taste

Sift buckwheat flour into pot. Scald it with boiling water. Sprinkle with salt and add egg. Mix well. Place dough on a floured board and roll it into ½-inch wide rope. Cut it into little pieces and cook covered in salted boiling water on low heat for 7-10 min. Transfer to colander and rinse with hot water. Drain and place in serving dish. Brown finely chopped onion in salt pork fat and serve *halushky* with onion gravy.

HALUSHKY FROM FARINA
ГАЛУШКИ БОРОШНЯНІ

½ qt. milk
1 stick butter
5 c. farina
½ c. sugar
3 eggs
3 T. grated almonds
½ t. grated lemon peel
1/3 c. powdered sugar
salt to taste

Bring milk to boil and add butter. Remove from heat and gradually add farina. Stir thoroughly with wooden spoon until smooth. Set aside for 10 min. Add sugar, eggs, salt, grated almonds and lemon peel and mix well. Drop dough by spoonfuls into boiling salted water. Cover and cook on slow boil for 5-7 min. When *halushky* rise, let them simmer for 3-5 min. Transfer to colander and rinse with hot water. Serve hot with melted butter.

APPLE HALUSHKY
ГАЛУШКИ ЯБЛУЧНІ

2 ½ lbs. apples
1/3 qt. milk
3 eggs
¼ c. sugar
1½ lbs. flour
½ stick butter
salt to taste

Cut peeled and cored apples into thin slices. Cover with milk and eggs whipped with salt and sugar. Gradually add flour and beat dough. Cook spoonfuls of dough in salted water at low boil until *halushky* are ready. Transfer to colander. Serve hot with melted butter.

HALUSHKY WITH HAM
СВИНЯЧІ ГАЛУШКИ

2 c. flour
1/3 c. milk
1 egg
2 T. butter
¼ lb. ham
salt to taste

Mix flour with milk. Stir in egg and sprinkle with salt. Knead batter. Transfer to wooden board. Roll it thin. Cut into squares 4 inch x 4 inch. Cook in boiling salted water for 10 min. Drain and cover with cold water. Drain and transfer into a baking pan. Add ham cut into small pieces. Drizzle with melted butter. Mix well and warm in a 350° oven for 5-7 min.

BREAD CRUMB HALUSHKY
ГАЛУШКИ З ХЛІБНИМИ ОКРУШИНКАМИ

2 eggs
1 T. sugar
1½ c. bread crumbs
¼ c. milk
4 T. melted butter
salt to taste

Mix eggs with sugar. Add bread crumbs, milk and half the melted butter. Sprinkle with salt and mix well. Set aside for 30 min. Drop by spoonfuls into boiling salted water. Take *halushky* out of water when they rise. Serve with melted butter.

DUMPLINGS (VARENIKY)

DUMPLINGS WITH FARMER CHEESE
ВАРЕНИКИ З СЕЛЯНСЬКИМ СИРОМ

1½ lbs. flour
1 c. milk
½ stick butter
3 eggs
2 T. sugar
salt to taste

For filling:
2 lbs. farmer cheese
½ c. sugar
¼ t. vanilla
¼ c. sour cream
2 eggs
½ stick butter
1/8 t. salt

Sift flour and add milk and melted butter. Stir well. Combine with eggs and add salt and sugar. Mix until smooth. Roll out thinly in a square. Set aside. *For filling*: Grind farmer cheese and add sugar, salt and vanilla. Stir well. Add sour cream and whipped eggs. Mix well. Form into walnut-sized balls. Divide square of dough into two rectangles. Line up balls on half of dough an inch from each other and about 2 inches from edges. Cover with the other part of dough. Press dough down around each ball and cut circles with a glass. Pinch edges together. Cook dumplings in salted boiling water for 7-10 min. When they rise take them out with slotted spoon. Drain well and place on a serving plate; drizzle with melted butter. Serve with sour cream and jam.

BAKED DUMPLINGS WITH CREAMED CHEESE
ВАРЕНИКИ ЗАПЕЧЕНЫЕ З СЕЛЯНСЬКИМ СИРОМ

½ t. yeast
1 c. water
1 egg
3 T. sugar
1 lb. flour

For filling:
1¾ lbs. farmer cheese
2 eggs
butter
1 c. sour cream
½ c. sugar
salt to taste

Dissolve yeast in cold water. Add egg, sugar and salt and stir well. Gradually stir in flour and knead well. Transfer to wooden board and roll dough out thinly. Cut it into squares, 2½ x 2½. Set aside. *For filling*: Grate about 1¼ lbs. farmer cheese. Add eggs, sugar and salt and mix thoroughly. Place spoonfuls of filling in the middle of dough squares, fold over and pinch. Leave dumplings in warm place for 15 min. Cook in salted boiling water for 8-10 min. Drain in colander. Transfer to baking pan and cover with remaining farmer cheese, melted butter, eggs and sour cream. Sprinkle with sugar. Bake in 350° oven for 10 min. Serve hot.

DUMPLINGS WITH MEAT FILLING
ВАРЕНИКИ З М'ЯСОМ

For dumplings:
2½ c. wheat flour
1 egg
¼ c. water
½ t. salt

For filling:
½ lb. fillet of beef, cooked
½ lb. fillet of pork, cooked
1 onion
1/3 stick butter or ¼ lb. salt pork

Mix flour, egg and water. Knead dough well. Roll out thinly in a square. Cut into circles with a glass. Set aside for 40 min. Cut up fillet of beef and pork into small pieces. Brown in butter. Stew with a little water. Pass stewed meat twice through meat-grinder. Add finely chopped onion. Sprinkle with salt and black pepper and mix well, adding 2-3 T. meat broth to hold mixture together. Place stuffing in the middle of each circle, fold over and pinch edges. Cook in salted boiling water for 8-10 min. Serve in a bowl with broth. Otherwise, transfer to colander. Drain. Place on serving plate and pour over melted butter or browned salt pork.

DUMPLINGS WITH MEAT AND CABBAGE FILLING
ВАРЕНИКИ З М'ЯСОМ ТА КАПУСТОЮ

For dumplings:
½ lb. flour
½ c. water
1 egg

For filling:
3 lbs. cabbage
½ lb. beef
½ lb. pork
2 onions
1/3 stick butter
salt and pepper to taste

Prepare dough as above: mix together flour, egg and water, knead well, roll dough out and cut into circles. Set aside for 40 min. Wash and cook cabbage. Grind it in meat-grinder. Cut up fillet of beef and pork into small pieces and brown them. Stew in a small amount of water. Grind stewed meat twice in meat-grinder. Add finely chopped onion, salt and black pepper and mix well. Combine with ground cabbage and mix well once again. Place stuffing in the middle of each circle. Fold over and pinch borders. Place in salted boiling water. Cook covered for 8-10 min. Test for readiness. Transfer to colander and drain. Place on a serving plate and pour over melted butter or browned salt pork. Or leave dumplings in liquid and serve with bouillon.

POPPY SEED DUMPLINGS
МАКОВІ ВАРЕНИКИ

1½ c. poppy seed
3 c. water
1½ c. sugar
3 T. powdered sugar or ¼ c. honey
salt to taste
1 recipe dough for dumplings

In pot, scald poppy seed with 1½ c. of boiling water. Drain and scald with the rest of boiling water. Warm on low heat for 15 min., not boiling. Drain and grind poppy seed with sugar to a powder. Place ground poppy seed and sugar into center of prepared dough circles. Fold over and pinch edges. Cook in boiling salted water right away. When dumplings rise, they are ready. Transfer to serving dish with slotted spoon. Sprinkle with powdered sugar or drizzle with honey. Delicious!

DUMPLINGS WITH CABBAGE AND MUSHROOMS
ВАРЕНИКИ З КАПУСТОЮ ТА ГРИБАМИ

½ c. dried mushrooms
½ lb. sauerkraut
¼ small head cabbage
2 onions
3 T. butter
salt and pepper to taste
1 recipe dough for dumplings

Wash, soak and cook dried mushrooms in water to cover. Finely chop cabbage, mix with sauerkraut and stew in butter and mushroom bouillon. Chop onions and brown in butter. Combine with cooked and finely chopped mushrooms and brown for 5-7 min. more. Mix all ingredients and sprinkle with salt and black pepper. Use as filling for halushky.

DUMPLINGS WITH FISH FILLING
ВАРЕНИКИ З РИБОЮ

For filling:
1 lb. fish fillet
3 onions
1/8 t. black pepper
3 pieces white bread
1 c. water
¼ c. oil
salt to taste
1 recipe dough for dumplings

Prepare dough as in preceding recipe. Finely chop fillet. Add 1 browned and chopped onion. Sprinkle with salt and pepper. Combine with white bread soaked in water. Grind mixture in meat grinder and use as filling for dumplings. Serve with additional onions browned in oil.

DUMPLINGS WITH CHERRIES
ВИШНЕВІ ВАРЕНИКИ

4 c. cherries
½ c. sugar
½ c. sour cream
salt to taste
1 recipe dough for dumplings

Place pitted cherries into a pot. Stir in sugar and let sit for 30 min. Meanwhile, prepare dough for dumplings. Drain juice from cherries and use it as beverage. Place cherries in circles cut from prepared dough. Pinch edges together. Place in boiling salted water. When dumplings are ready, they will rise. Transfer to serving dish with spoon. Pour over sour cream. Serve with prepared juice. A traditional Ukrainian hit!

DUMPLINGS WITH LIVER FILLING
ВАРЕНИКИ З ПЕЧІНКОЮ

1 lb. beef liver
¼ lb. salt pork
2 onions
1 bay leaf
1/3 stick butter
salt and pepper to taste
1 recipe dough for dumplings

Prepare dough as above. Wash and clean liver. Cut prepared liver and salt pork into small cubes. Cook with onion and bay leaf for 30 min. Grind in meat-grinder. Add finely chopped browned onion, salt and black pepper and mix well. Form and cook dumplings as in previous recipes. Serve with melted butter.

DUMPLINGS WITH POTATO FILLING
ВАРЕНИКИ З КАРТОПЛЕЮ

5 potatoes
¼ lb. onions
1/5 lb. salt pork
1/8 t. black pepper
salt to taste
1 recipe dough for dumplings

Wash and cook potatoes while you prepare dough for dumplings. Peel potatoes under cold running water. Mash thoroughly. Add chopped onion browned in salt pork. Sprinkle with pepper. Mix well until smooth. Roll out dough and cut into round dumplings with glass. Place potato-onion filling in the middle of each circle, pinch edges together to seal. Drop dumplings into salted boiling water. Cook for 5-7 min. Drain and transfer to serving plate. Serve hot with browned salt pork cracklings.

DUMPLINGS WITH POTATO AND
MUSHROOM FILLING
ВАРЕНИКИ З КАРТОПЛЕЮ И ГРЫБАМИ

For filling:
¼ lb. mushrooms
½ lb. potatoes
1 onion
2 T. sunflower oil
salt and pepper to taste
1 recipe dough for dumplings

For gravy:
5 T. sunflower oil
1 onion

Prepare dough and cut into squares (about 2½ x 2½). Set aside. Wash, finely chop and boil mushrooms. Cook, peel and mash potatoes. Mix mashed potatoes with chopped boiled mushrooms. Place spoonful mixture in the middle of each square. Fold over to make triangles and pinch edges together to seal. Cook as above. Serve with chopped onions browned in oil.

DUMPLINGS WITH LUNG FILLING
ВАРЕНИКИ З СВИНЯЧИМИ ЛЕГЕНЯМИ

1 lb. pork or veal lungs and heart
3 onions
1 bay leaf
salt to taste
2-3 peppercorns
1/3 stick butter
1 recipe dough for dumplings

Prepare dough as above. Wash and clean lungs and heart. Cut into cubes. Place in a pot and scald with boiling water. Cook for 15-20 min. Drain. Add water, 1 onion, pepper, salt and bay leaf. Cook covered for 20-30 min. Drain. Grind in meat-grinder together with 1 slightly browned onion. Mix well. Form and cook dumplings as in preceding recipe. Garnish with fried chopped onions and serve with melted butter or vinegar.

EGG DISHES

EGGS IN SOUR CREAM
ЯЙЦЯ В СМЕТАНІ

10 eggs, boiled
1½ c. sour cream
1 t. butter
salt to taste

Cut boiled eggs into quarters. Place in buttered pan. Sprinkle with salt. Cover with sour cream and bake in a 325° oven for 20 min.

FRIED EGGS WITH ONION
СМАЖЕНІ ЯЙЦЯ З ЦИБУЛЕЮ

½ onion
2 t. butter
5 eggs
salt to taste

Brown finely chopped onion in butter. Break fresh eggs over onions. Sprinkle with salt and fry.

GUTZUL SCRAMBLED EGGS
ГУТЦУЛЬСЬКІЕ БИТІ ЯЙЦЯ

1 c. heavy cream
1 c. sour cream
1 c. corn flour
4 eggs
3 T. butter
1 T. chopped fresh parsley
salt to taste

Combine heavy cream with sour cream. Stir in corn flour, add eggs, sprinkle with salt and mix well. Fry by spoonfuls in hot butter. Sprinkle with parsley before serving.

SCRAMBLED EGGS WITH BREAD CRUMBS
БИТІ ЯЙЦЯ З ХЛІБНИМИ ОКРУШИНКАМИ

1 T. bread crumbs
2 T. butter
5 eggs
salt to taste

Brown bread crumbs in butter. Pour over whipped eggs. Sprinkle with salt. Place in 325° oven and bake for 5 min.

OMELET WITH MEAT STUFFING
ОМЛЕТ З М'ЯСНИМ ФАРШЕМ

4 eggs
¼ c. milk
1 pinch salt
¼ lb. ham
½ lb. liver
¼ lb. sausage
3 t. butter
1 tomato

Whip eggs with milk and salt. Fry omelet in hot butter. Finely cut ham, cooked liver and sausage. Fry in another pan for 3-5 min. Place in center of omelet and warm on low heat for 2-3 min. Transfer to serving plate and decorate with slices of tomatoes.

OMELET WITH FARMER CHEESE
ОМЛЕТ З СЕЛЯНСЬКИМ СИРОМ

5 eggs
¼ c. milk
¼ lb. farmer cheese
1 t. flour
1 T. butter

Whip eggs with milk and salt. Mix with grated farmer cheese. Add flour and mix well. Pour into hot skillet with butter and bake in a 325° oven for 7-10 min. Serve hot.

EGGS WITH MUSHROOMS
ЯЄЧНА ЗАПІКАНКА З ГРИБАМИ

6 mushrooms
1 onion
4 T. butter
10 eggs, boiled

For gravy:
2 T. flour
2 T. butter
1 c. milk
salt and pepper to taste

Clean and wash mushrooms. Cook them for 10-15 min., then fry with chopped onion and butter. Combine with boiled eggs cut into quarters and place in casserole. Brown flour in butter for milk gravy. Constantly stirring flour add milk. Sprinkle with salt and bring to boil. Season with salt and pepper and pour over eggs and mushrooms. Bake in a 325° oven for 7-10 min.

DESSERT DISHES

HONEY COOKIES
МЕДОВІ ПРЯНИКИ

2½ c. flour
3 egg yolks
1 c. sugar
2 T. butter
4 T. honey
1 t. baking soda
1 t. cinnamon
1 t. ground cloves
peel of 1 lemon
1 pinch salt

Mix flour with melted butter. Stir egg yolks and sugar. Combine with flour. Add honey, soda, cloves and cinnamon. Sprinkle with grated lemon peel. Mix thoroughly. Roll out ¼ inch thick. Cut into squares. Place on greased baking sheet. Bake in preheated 350° oven 15 min.

CHEESECAKE WITH ALMONDS
СИРНИЙ ПИРІГ З МИГДАЛЕМ

1 lb. farmer cheese
2 T. farina
4 T. butter
1 t. vanilla
½ c. crushed almonds
4 eggs
¾ c. sugar
½ c. sweet cloves
pinch salt
fruit syrup or preserves

Grate farmer's cheese. Mix with farina, melted butter and vanilla. Add crushed almonds and egg yolks beaten with sugar until they are light. Stir in cloves. Mix again. Place in a greased baking pan and bake in preheated 350° oven for 55 min. Serve hot with fruit syrup or with preserves.

UKRAINIAN PUDDING
ТІСТЕЧКО МИГДАЛЕВЕ

1 c. bread crumbs
1 qt. milk
4 eggs
1 c. brown sugar
1 grated lemon rind
¼ c. chopped almonds
3 T. butter
1 pinch salt

Soak bread crumbs in milk ½ hour. Beat yolks well with sugar. Add soaked crumbs, lemon rind, almonds and beaten egg whites. Grease molds with butter. Place batter in the molds. Bake in 350° oven for 35 min. or until firm.

CHEESE CAKE
СИРНИЙ ПИРІГ

1 cake yeast
2 c. milk
4 c. flour
1 stick butter

For filling:
3 eggs
1 c. sugar
2 lbs. farmer cheese, grated

Stir yeast in warm milk. Gradually add half flour. Stir well. Set aside for 3 hrs. to rise. When it doubles, add the second half of flour. Stir well and knead on a floured board or table. Set aside for 2 hrs. to rise. Roll out 2 inches thick. Place on well greased sheet. *For filling:* Stir beaten eggs with sugar and farmer cheese. Spread cheese filling over the dough evenly. Roll up edges. Brush with lightly beaten egg white. Cover with cloth. Set aside for 15 min. to rise in warm place. Transfer to oven. Bake in 350° for 30-40 min.

APPLE CAKE
ЯБЛУЧНИЙ ПИРІГ

3 c. flour
1 c. sugar
½ lb. butter
½ t. baking soda
1 c. yogurt
1 egg
¼ c. bread crumbs or farina

For filling:
3 lbs. apples
1 c. sugar
vanilla to taste

Mix flour, sugar, butter and soda. Add yogurt, egg and beat batter. Spread 2/3 in ¼ inch thick rectangle. Sprinkle with bread crumbs or farina and transfer to well buttered pan. Core and thinly slice apples. Sprinkle with sugar and let set for half an hour. Drain off excess juice. Season with vanilla. Spread evenly on dough. Cut strips from the rest of dough and arrange in lattice on top. Brush with beaten egg. Bake in 375° oven for 40 min.

APPLE STRUDEL
ЯБЛУЧНИЙ ШТРУДЕЛЬ

3 c. flour
2 eggs
4 T. oil
½ salt
1 c. water
1 t. powdered sugar
3 T. raisins
¼ t. vanilla

For filling:
1 lb. apples
2 T. sugar
½ bread crumbs
¼ t. cinnamon

Mix flour, eggs and salt. Add half the oil and knead dough well. Cover with cloth. Set aside in warm place for 2 hrs. to rise. Roll out ½ inch thick. Brush with oil and transfer to flour-dusted towel. Stretch dough with aid of towel, so that it becomes evenly thin. Set aside for 15 min. Dot it with oil. *For filling:* Wash and cut apples into wedges. Sprinkle with sugar, cinnamon and bread crumbs. Spread them on a half of the dough. Roll it up with aid of towel but not too tightly. Decorate top with raisins. Brush with beaten egg and melted butter. Make slits in top. Transfer to a greased baking pan and bake in 375° oven for 50 min. Reduce heat to 350° and brush with more butter if it browns too quickly. Dust with powdered sugar before serving.

APPLE PANCAKE
ЯБЛУЧНІ МЛИНЧИКИ

1 stick butter
2 eggs
2 T. sugar
2 c. flour
6 apples
peel of 1 lemon
1 t. salt
2 T. bread crumbs
4 T. powdered sugar

Beat together ½ stick butter, egg yolks and sugar. Mix in flour, 1 c. at a time until batter is smooth. Add grated lemon peel, salt and mix. Fold in beaten egg whites and mix well. Roll out dough. Even it up. Divide in 2 parts. Transfer one to greased frying pan. Sprinkle with crumbs. Slice cored apples. Sprinkle with sugar. Spread over dough. Cover with the second rectangle. Fry on both sides. Sprinkle pancake with powdered sugar.

PEACH AND PEAR SALAD
САЛАТ З ПЕРСИКІВ ТА ГРУШ

1 lb. peaches and pears
½ c. powdered sugar
juice of 1 lemon

Wash peaches and pears. Pit and core and cut up. Mix with powdered sugar and lemon juice.

SLYVOVNYK PIE
СЛИВОВНИК

1 cake yeast
1 T. brown sugar
1 c. milk
4 c. flour
3 eggs
2 T. powdered sugar
¼ t. salt
1 T. vodka or other alcohol
½ c. butter

For filling:
1 lb. plums
½ c. brown sugar
1 t. cinnamon
¼ t. saffron
1/3 c. plum jam
1 T. vodka or other alcohol

Mash yeast with brown sugar. Stir in warm milk. Add 1 c. flour and mix well. Cover with cloth and leave in warm place for 30 min. Whip 2 egg yolks and 1 whole egg with powdered sugar. Combine 3 c. flour with egg mixture and sponge. Add salt and vodka. Knead well until dough is smooth. Add small pieces butter and keep kneading until dough doesn't stick to hands. Cover and set aside in warm place to raise. When double in bulk, roll out ½ inch thick circle with raised edges. Refrigerate. *For filling:* wash, cut and pit plums and arrange on dough 2 inch from edges. Mix sugar, cinnamon, saffron and vodka with plum jam and spread over plums. Transfer to generously buttered pan. Bake in 350° oven for 45-50 min., or until crust becomes light brown.

PUMPKIN PIE WITH HONEY
ГАРБУЗОВИЙ ПИРІГ З МЕДОМ

2 c. *whole wheat flour*
¼ t. *salt*
1 t. *brown sugar*
¾ c. *butter*
1 t. *sunflower oil*
¼ c. *water*

For filling:
1 *small sweet pumpkin*
3 *eggs*
1 *egg yolk*
1 c. *cream*
3 ½ T. *brown sugar*
1 t. *rum or vodka*
1 t. *ginger*
2 T *honey*
1 t. *ground cinnamon*
2 T. *butter*

Mix flour, sugar and salt. Add half of the butter, mix well. Dice the remaining butter into very small pieces before adding; add sunflower oil and let sit for a while. Sprinkle the dough with water, one tablespoon at a time, cutting with knife between additions. Draw dough together, then divide into two parts. Roll out each ½ inch thick. *For filling:* Cut pumpkin into three or four pieces, remove seeds. Bake approx. 60 min. Remove skin. Make puree from pumpkin (approx. 1½ c.). Add remaining ingredients and honey. Mix well. Roll each pastry disk to 12-inch diameter, raise sides to form a "plate." Chill ½ hour. Preheat oven to 350°. Bake 15 min. Reduce heat. Bake for 15 more min., until the bottom becomes dry. Fill with pumpkin filling. Bake for 45 min. Serve hot.

APPLE DESSERT
ЯБЛУЧНИЙ ДЕСЕРТ

1 lb. green apples
10 walnuts
½ c. powdered sugar
¼ c. heavy cream
¼ t. vanilla to taste

Wash and cut up apples. Core and grate. Chop walnuts and combine with grated apples. Mix and sprinkle with powdered sugar and vanilla. Pour over whipped cream.

PEACH AND PLUM SALAD
САЛАТ СЛИВОПЕРСИКОВИЙ

1 lb. peaches and plums
½ c. powdered sugar
10 walnuts
¼ c. heavy cream
¼ c. vanilla

Wash and cut up peaches and plums. Take out pits and cut into small pieces. Mix with chopped walnuts, powdered sugar and vanilla. Top with whipped cream.

APRICOT SALAD
АБРИКОСОВИЙ САЛАТ

1 lb. apricots
3 T. powdered sugar
½ glass rosé wine

Wash and peel apricots. Cut into small pieces. Pour over wine. Sprinkle with powdered sugar.

ASSORTED FRUIT SALAD
ФРУХТОВИЙ САЛАТ

½ lb. seedless grapes
¼ lb. plums
¼ lb. apples
¼ lb. pears
1 lemon
4 T. powdered sugar

Wash and pit/core and cut up fruits. Dice them. Mix with grapes and finely chopped walnuts. Pour over lemon juice, sprinkle with powdered sugar.

STRAWBERRIES IN CUSTARD SAUCE
СУНИЧНИЙ САЛАТ З МОЛОКОМ

2 lbs. strawberries
½ c. sugar
3 eggs
1 t. starch
1½ c. milk
vanilla to taste

Mix strawberries with sugar. Dissolve starch in a little warm water. Mix egg yolks with starch, sugar and vanilla, then add whipped egg whites. Put in double boiler or improvise with one pot in another pot of boiling water. Stir the mixture while water is simmering, gradually adding hot milk until sauce thickens. Set pot of thickened sauce into cold water and continue whipping until totally chilled. Serve strawberries with prepared sauce.

CHERRIES WITH SUGAR AND SOUR CREAM
ВИШНІ З ЦУКРОМ ТА СМЕТАНОЮ

1 lb. cherries
1 c. sugar
3 c. sour cream

Wash cherries. Take out pits. Sprinkle with sugar and top with sour cream.

APPLES WITH CHEESE STUFFING
ЯБЛУКА З СИРОМ

1 lb. apples
1/3 lb. farmer cheese
1 egg
1½ T. sugar
¾ c. fruit or berry syrup

Wash and peel apples. Slice in half. Core and stuff with grated farmer cheese mixed with raw egg and sugar. Place prepared apples in casserole sprinkled with water. Bake in 325° in oven for 10-15 min. until tender. Serve baked apples with fruit or berry syrup.

APRICOTS STUFFED WITH NUTS AND CREAM
АБРИКОСИ З ГОРІХАМИ ПІД СМЕТАНОЮ

20 apricots
1 c. grated walnuts or hazelnuts
1 pt. whipped cream or sour cream
3 T. powdered sugar
3-4 T. grated chocolate

Wash apricots and pit. Cook until half-ready. Drain, sweeten and save liquid for beverage. Fill apricots with grated walnuts or hazelnuts. Place in dish lightly dusted with powdered sugar. Stir whipped cream or sour cream with powdered sugar into froth. Cover stuffed apricots with whipped cream and sprinkle with grated chocolate.

CHERRY CAKE
ВИШНЕВИЙ ПИРІГ

1 cake yeast
1 c. milk
1 t. sugar
3 eggs
1 t. powdered sugar
1 t. vanilla
3 cups flour
1/3 cup sweet butter

For filling:
2 lbs. ripe cherries
2 oz. cranberry juice, lemon juice or fruit nectar
1 c. sugar
¼ t. cinnamon

Dissolve yeast in 1 c. warm milk. Add 1 t. sugar. Mix. Put aside in warm place for 15 min. Beat 1 egg and 2 yolks with sugar and vanilla. Add melted butter, yeast and salt to mixture. Constantly stirring, pour in flour. Knead dough until it doesn't stick to hands. Cover with cloth and set aside in warm place to rise. When it doubles in bulk, divide it in two parts. Roll out ½ inch thick in circle. Transfer dough to a well greased pan. *For filling*: Remove pits from cherries. Mix sugar with spice and juice, add to cherries and mix again. Brush one disk of the dough with beaten egg whites. Pour the filling on the pastry "plate." Cover with the second disk. Press edges together. Bake in 375° oven for 40-50 min. Serve warm. This cake is best the day it is baked.

SUMMER FRUIT CAKE
СОЛОДКИЙ ЛІТНІЙ ПИРІГ З ФРУКТАМИ

3 c. flour
1 c. sugar
½ lb. butter
½ t. baking soda
2 T. water
1 c. sour cream
1 egg
1 lb. berries or 2 lbs. fruit
1 c. powdered sugar

Mix flour, sugar, butter and soda. Add water, sour cream, and egg and beat dough well. Roll it out into a circle ¼ inch thick. Arrange strawberries, raspberries, blueberries and cherries in layer, pitted and cut plums or thinly sliced pitted peaches or apricots. Sprinkle with powdered sugar. Transfer to generously buttered pan. Bake in 350° oven 35-45 min. Cool and serve.

MEDOVYK
МЕДОВИК

1 c. honey
¼ c oil
1 c. sugar
3 eggs
¼ c. rum
1/3 t. cinnamon
¼ t. ground cloves
2 c. flour
½ c. milk
1 T. baking soda
2 T. water
¼ c. hazelnuts or raisins

Mix well honey, oil and sugar until smooth. Add whipped eggs, continuously beating. Season with rum, cinnamon and ground cloves. Continuously beating, gradually sift in flour. Gradually add milk and stir well. Add soda dissolved in water. Knead well. Transfer dough to a well greased and floured loaf pan filling it ¾ full. Brush top with water and decorate with split hazelnuts or raisins. Bake in 350° oven for 35-45 min. If top browns too quickly, cover with aluminum foil. Check with wooden pick. When it comes out clean, it is ready. Set aside in room temperature overnight.

SMETANNYK
СМЕТАННИК

5 egg yolks
2 c. sugar
2 c. sour cream
2 c. flour
½ c. cocoa
½ c. sugar
1 lemon
4 T. powdered sugar
½ t. vanilla

Stir egg yolks with sugar and sour cream until mixture becomes smooth. Gradually stir in flour. Combine cocoa with sugar and add to egg mixture. Season with grated lemon peel. Knead well. Transfer to generously greased and floured pan. Bake in 350° oven for 35-45 min. Set aside to cool. Sprinkle with powdered sugar and vanilla before serving.

NUTS & APPLES PIE
ПИРІГ З ГОРІХАМИ ТА ЯБЛУКАМИ

¼ lb. lard
¼ t. lemon juice
2 eggs
2 ½ c. flour
¼ t. baking soda
½ c. hazelnuts
2 ½ c. sugar
1 t. vanilla

For filling:
3-4 apples
½ c. powdered sugar
cinnamon to taste

Stir together lemon juice and lard. Combine with whipped egg yolks. Gradually add flour and baking soda. Mix well. Add ground hazelnuts, sugar and vanilla. Knead dough until it is thick and elastic. Transfer ¾ dough to greased pan. *For filling*: Grate apples and spread in layers on dough. Sprinkle with powdered sugar and cinnamon. Cut rest of dough in thin strips. Place them on top in a lattice. Brush with egg whites beaten to froth. Bake in 375° oven for 35-45 min.

CHOCOLATE CAKE POLTAVA-STYLE
ПОЛТАВСЬКИЙ ШОКОЛАДНИЙ ПИРІГ

1½ sticks butter
½ c. sugar
4 eggs
2 c. flour
3 oz. bar of chocolate
1/3 c. raspberry jam
½ c. grated chocolate
¼ c. grated walnuts

Whip butter and combine with egg yolks and ¼ c. sugar. Gradually add flour. Mix and combine with melted chocolate and egg whites whipped with ¼ c. sugar. Beat well. Transfer batter to greased and floured baking pan. The height of the dough should not exceed ½ inch. Bake in 350° oven 30-40 min. Spread raspberry jam over hot cake and sprinkle with grated chocolate and walnuts.

CHEESE-APPLE BABKA
БАБКА СИРНО-ЯБЛУЧНА

1 lb. farmer cheese
¼ t. salt
3 T. sugar
1 lb. apples
½ c. bread crumbs
2 eggs
1 T. butter
½ c. berry syrup

Grate farmer cheese. Add salt and sugar. Mix with peeled
and grated apples. Sprinkle with bread crumbs. Add egg
yolks. Whip egg whites and fold in. Use double boiler or
pan inside a larger pot with hot water. Grease bottom of
pan and cover it with thick layer of crumbs before you
pour in batter. Simmer covered in "water bath" for 30 min.
Serve with berry syrup.

CHEESE-CARROT BABKA
СИРНО-МОРКВЯНА БАБКА

1 lb. farmer cheese
2 eggs
½ c. sugar
2 T. vanilla
5 carrots
4 T. bread crumbs
2 T. butter
1 c. heavy cream

Grate farmer cheese. Mix with fresh egg yolks, sugar, and vanilla. Add carrots ground in meat grinder and stewed with butter. Combine with whipped egg whites. Mix well and sprinkle with bread crumbs. Transfer to a pot well greased and thickly covered with crumbs. Place in a larger pot with hot water. Simmer covered in "water bath" for 45-50 min. Serve with whipped cream.

BEVERAGES

EGGNOG WITH HONEY
ЯЄЧНА НУГА З МЕДОМ

3 c. milk
3 egg yolks
6 T. honey
3 T. lemon or orange juice

Mix together egg yolks, cold milk, honey and lemon or orange juice. Whip until blended together.

HONEY-LEMON DRINK
МЕДОВО-ЛИМОННИЙ НАПІЙ

3 qts. water
8 T. honey
2 lemons
2-3 T. sugar

Bring water to boil and cool. Add sugar and honey. Peel lemons, squeeze juice from them and add the juice as well as cut up lemon peel to beverage. Let stand. Filter, pour in bottles and cork. Refrigerate for 1 hour or more. Serve cool.

EGGNOG DESSERT WITH NUTMEG
ЯЄІЧНА НУҐА З ГОРІХАМИ

4 eggs
4 T. sugar
½ c. strawberry or cherry juice
½ c. cold boiled water
2 c. cold milk
3 t. nutmeg
salt to taste

Whip egg yolks to froth. Add sugar and either strawberry or cherry juice. Mix well. Dissolve with cold milk and cold boiled water. Mix again. Whip egg whites to froth and fold into prepared mixture. Sprinkle with grated nutmeg and serve in tall glasses.

MILK-AND-WALNUT DRINK
МОЛОЧНО-ГОРІХОВИЙ НАПІЙ

½ lb. walnuts
3 c. milk
3 T. sugar

Pulverize walnuts. Dissolve sugar in chilled milk. Mix in crushed walnuts. Simmer for 10-15 min. to develop flavor and then chill.

MILK-AND-PEACH DRINK
МОЛОЧНО-ПЕРСИКОВИЙ НАПІЙ

4 peaches
1 c. orange juice
4 c. milk

Whip together peeled and finely cut up peaches, orange juice and cold milk. Serve in tall goblets.

MILK-RASPBERRY-AND-APPLE DRINK
МОЛОЧНО-МАЛИНОВИЙ НАПІЙ

4 apples
1 container of raspberries
4 c. milk

Peel and cut apples and core. Mix apples with crushed raspberries. Add milk and blend. Can be served with whipped cream.

MILK-AND-RASPBERRY DRINK
WITH ICE CREAM
МОЛОЧНО-МАЛИНОВИЙ НАПІЙ З МОРОЗИВОМ

4 c. milk
½ c. raspberry syrup
1 c. vanilla ice-cream
4 raspberries

Whip milk with raspberry syrup. Serve in glasses with vanilla or pistachio ice-cream and raspberries as garnish.

MILK-AND-ORANGE DRINK WITH EGG YOLKS
МОЛОЧНО-АПЕЛЬСИНОВИЙ НАПІЙ З ЯЄЧНИМИ ЖОВТКАМИ

4 egg yolks
2 c. milk
1 c. orange juice

Whip egg yolks with milk and orange juice. Can be served with whipped cream.

CARROT-AND-ICE-CREAM DRINK
НАПІЙ МОРКВА З МОРОЗИВОМ

2 c. carrot juice
2 c. vanilla ice cream

Whip carrot juice and vanilla ice cream together. Serve chilled.

MILK-AND-CELERY DRINK WITH CHEESE
МОЛОЧНИЙ НАПІЙ З СЕЛЕРОЮ ТА СИРОПОМ

4 egg yolks
2 c. celery juice
3 T. lemon juice
2 c. milk
4 t. grated cheese

Whip egg yolk, celery juice, lemon juice and cold milk. Sprinkle with grated cheese and serve.

YOGURT-AND-BEET DRINK
БУРЯКОВА РЯЖАНКА

2 c. yogurt
1 c. beet juice
2 t. chopped dill
sugar, salt and pepper to taste

Whip chilled yogurt. Gradually add beet juice and finely chopped dill. Season with salt, sugar and black pepper.

APPLE DRINK
ЯБЛУЧНИЙ НАПІЙ

3 lbs. apples
2 qts. water
2 lemons
1 c. sugar

Peel apples and cut them up finely. Place in jar. Pour over warm boiled water. Squeeze lemons. Add finely chopped lemon peels and sugar. For rich taste, let stand covered for 12 hrs.

CHERRY DRINK
ВИШНЕВИЙ НАПІЙ

1 c. cherry juice
8 t. sugar
3 c. boiling water
½ lemon

Combine water, sugar, cherry juice and lemon juice. Bring to boil. Serve drink when chilled.

STRAWBERRY DRINK
СУНИЧНИЙ НАПІЙ

1 lb. strawberries
4 c. water
1 lemon
3 t. sugar

Crush ¾ c. strawberries to extract juice. Collect it. Cover pulp with water. Bring to boil. Add sugar. Boil for 5-7 min. Set aside. Squeeze lemon. Combine all ingredients and add a few lemon slices to boiled mixture. Cool and serve.

CRANBERRY DRINK
КЛЮКВЯНИЙ НАПІЙ

½ c. cranberries
3 c. water
2 T. sugar
½ c. honey
½ lemon

Crush cranberries with wooden spoon. Collect juice. Pour hot water over pulp and boil for 3-4 min. Add sugar and honey and bring to boil. Strain boiled mixture. Add cranberry juice and juice of lemon. Serve chilled.

LEMONADE
ЛИМОНАД

10 c. water
5 lemons
2 c. sugar

Wash lemons with hot water. Peel with knife. Cover skins with cold water and bring to boil. Strain. Combine 1 c. cold water and sugar. Bring to boil. Squeeze lemons. Collect juice. Combine with strained lemon water and sugar syrup. Set aside. Before serving, add diced peeled lemon for taste and additional vitamins.

HEALTH DRINK
ЗДОРОВИЙ НАПІЙ

1 c. rose hips
½ lb. honey
4 t. sugar
3 c. water
lemon juice to taste

Wash rose hips with cold water. Cover with boiling water and boil for 5-7 . Add sugar and honey and lemon juice and boil for 3-4 min. Let sit for one day. Strain mixture and serve chilled.

HONEY-CHERRY DRINK
МЕДО-ВИШНЕВИЙ НАПІЙ

1 c. cherry juice
7 c. water
3 T. sugar
4 T. honey
2 c. water (for syrup)

Combine cherry juice with water. Dissolve sugar in water. Bring to boil. Add honey to sugar syrup. Combine with cherry liquid. Serve chilled.

MELON-WATERMELON DRINK
НАПІЙ З ДИНІ ТА КАВУНА

8 T. sugar
3 c. water
1 lemon
1 lb. watermelon and melon pulp

Dissolve sugar and lemon juice in hot water. Bring to boil. Put aside. Add melon, and watermelon cut in cubes. Set aside for 30 min. Strain drink. Serve chilled in tall glasses.

COFFEE DRINK
КАВОВИЙ НАПІЙ

4 c. coffee
2 T. sugar
1 c. plum syrup
lemon juice to taste

Chill coffee with added sugar. Combine with plum syrup. Add lemon juice. Serve in tall glasses.

ENERGY DRINK
МІЦНИЙ НАПІЙ

8 c. coffee
2 T. sugar
2 c. water
½ c. honey
½ c. mineral water
lemon juice and almond flavoring to taste

Combine sugar with water and bring to boil. Mix with coffee, mineral water and honey. Season with lemon juice and almond flavoring. Serve with wedges of lemon.

UKRAINIAN DRINK
УКРАЇНСЬКИЙ НАПІЙ

4 t. dried mint
4 c. water (for tea)
1 c. water (for syrup)
2 T. sugar
3 c. bread kvas
lemon juice to taste

Brew dried mint with boiling water. Set aside. Bring water to boil with sugar added. Set aside sugar syrup. Combine mint tea, sugar syrup and bread kvas. Strain and add lemon juice. Serve chilled.

BEER DRINK
ПИВОЧАЙ

2 c. beer
2 c. chilled tea
2 T. sugar
2 lemons

Brew tea. Strain and chill. Add beer and sugar. Squeeze lemon and serve with a lemon wedge in beer glasses.

SQUASH DRINK
ГАРБУЗОВИЙ НАПІЙ

4 c. squash juice
4 egg yolks
4 t. sugar
4 T. lemon juice
¼ t. ground peppercorns
4 T. whipped cream
salt to taste

Wash, clean, grate and squeeze squash. Mix with egg yolks. Add salt, sugar, lemon juice and ground peppercorns. Stir together. Serve with whipped cream.

VEGETABLE DRINK
ОВОЧЕВИЙ НАПІЙ

5 carrots
2 beets
2 c. water
1 lemon
2 t. honey
salt to taste

Wash, peel and grate beets and carrots. Pour over a little cold water. Mix and strain. Squeeze juice of lemon. Add honey. Stir and serve.

FARMER'S DRINK
СЕЛЯНСЬКИЙ НАПІЙ

1½ c. carrot juice
2 c. apple juice
½ c boiled water
2 T. onion juice
2 T. sugar
pinch salt

Mix carrot and apple juice. Add cold boiled water, juice of onion. Sprinkle with salt and sugar.

BEET DRINK
БУРЯКОВИЙ НАПІЙ

1 lb. beets
2 c. water
1 lemon
1 c. apple juice

For syrup:
4 T. sugar
1 c water

Grate washed and peeled beets. Add lemon juice squeezed from lemon. Pour over cold water, bring to boil, chill and strain. Boil water with sugar. Add sugar syrup and apple juice to beet liquid. Serve chilled.

BEET KVAS
БУРЯКОВИЙ КВАС

4 c. beet kvas
¼ lb. rye bread
4 t. sugar
horseradish
4 t. chopped dill
4 t. chopped scallion
4 T. whipped cream
salt to taste

Wash and peel beets. Cut into quarters. Cover with chilled boiled water. Add a few crusts of rye bread. Set aside in a warm place for 2-3 days. Strain and cool kvas. Add sugar and salt. Add grated horseradish and finely chopped dill and scallion. Serve chilled with whipped cream.

STRAWBERRY DESSERT DRINK
СУНИЧНИЙ ДЕСЕРТНИЙ НАПІЙ

2 oz. strawberries
1 oz. sugar syrup
½ lemon
4 oz. soda
ice
For syrup:
1 t. sugar
1 oz. water

Wash strawberries. Cut up and place in a glass. Bring to boil water with sugar for syrup. Combine with strawberries, lemon juice and a little soda. Serve with ice.

EGG TEA
ЯЄЧНИЙ ЧАЙ

4 t. tea leaves
2 egg whites
4 egg yolks
4 T. sugar
1 lemon

Pour hot water into tea kettle to warm it, Then empty. Place tea into warmed tea kettle. Fill 2/3 of it with boiling water. Set it aside for 5-7 min. covered with a napkin or towel to let it brew strong. Divide egg whites from yolks. Stir yolks with sugar. Beat mixture. Whip egg whites and mix with whipped egg yolks. Add lemon juice and whip the resulting mixture. Mix with 4 cups of tea and whip again. Pour liquid into warm cups. Delicious!

COCOA WITH EGG YOLKS
ШОКОЛАД З ЯЄЧНИМИ ЖОВТКАМИ

4 t. cocoa
8 t. sugar
3 c. milk
4 fresh egg yolks
whipped cream

Place cocoa in pot. Mix with sugar. Pour in a little hot milk or water and stir it thoroughly. Pour in the rest of hot milk constantly stirring. Bring to boil. Stir egg yolks with sugar and add to hot cocoa. Whip before serving with whipped cream.

KVAS FROM DRY BREAD
ХЛІБНИЙ КВАС

2 ½ lbs. rye bread
6 qts. water
1 T. yeast
1 c. sugar
½ c. raisins

Cut rye bread in slices. Brown them in oven. Place in pot. Pour over boiling water. Cover with a clean cloth. Set aside for 3-4 hrs. Strain liquid. Add dissolved yeast and sugar. Cover. Set aside for 5 hrs. until foam appears. Strain. Pour in bottles with a few raisins in each. Cork bottles. Tie each cork with string. Put bottles on sides in a chilly place for 2-3 days. Uncork and drink as much as you want. It is tasty and refreshing. Can also be used as base for cold soups.

ZAPORIZKY KVAS
ЗАПОРІЗЬКИЙ КВАС

2 ½ lbs. dry bread
7 qts. water
1 T. yeast
1 c. sugar
½ lemon
½ c. raisins

Pour boiling water in large pot or small barrel over dry bread. Put it aside for 7-8 hrs., covered with a clean cloth. Strain it and transfer to another pot. Add sugar and dissolved yeast. Mix and add lemon slices. Set aside for 7-8 hrs. more. Strain kvas and transfer into bottles with 3-5 raisins in each. Cork them well. Tie with string and put in warm place for 12 hrs. When kvas bubbles, move to a chilly place and store there.

DIET DRINK
ДІЄТИЧНИЙ НАПІЙ

2 c. yogurt
2 c. prune juice
3 T. sugar syrup (containing 6 t. sugar, ¾ c. water)

Prepare sugar syrup by mixing sugar in water and bringing to boil, then cool. Whip yogurt together with juice and sugar syrup.

COSSACK KVAS
КОЗАЦЬКИЙ КВАС

2 lbs. rye crackers
10 qts. boiling water
1 T. flour
1/3 c. yeast
1 lb. sugar
1 lemon

Pour boiling water over rye crackers. Set aside for 7-8 hrs. Dissolve flour and yeast in a cup of cracker infusion. Set aside for 10-15 min. to allow it to ferment. Strain cracker infusion through sieve. Add sugar. Pour in liquid with yeast and flour. Mix well. Set aside in warm place overnight. Ladle once more into bottles. Cut lemon in slices and add to bottles. Cork them. Tie with string. Set aside to cool. Store in a cold place.

KVAS BROVARSKY
БРОВАРСЬКИЙ КВАС

4 c. beer
7 qts. boiling water
¾ lb. sugar
½ c. raisins
½ lemon
1 T. yeast

Combine boiling water and beer in large pot. Squeeze juice from lemon. Add sugar, raisins and lemon peel. Mix and cover with cloth. Set aside for 4-5 hrs. Dissolve yeast in ½ c. warm water and pour into beer mixture. Set aside in a warm place. When it starts bubbling strongly, strain it. Ladle into bottles with a few raisins each. Seal tightly. When foam appears again, store in chilly place. Kvas becomes ready for use in 24 hrs.

HONEY BEER ANOTHER WAY
МЕДОВЕ ПИВО ПО-ІНШОМ

3 lbs. honey
1 egg white
6 qts. water
5 cloves
slice of ginger root
piece of cinnamon
1 t. yeast

Stir honey and egg white together. Transfer to large pot with boiling water. Add ginger, cloves and cinnamon and simmer on low heat for 1 hr. Remove from fire when ¼ of liquid evaporates and mixture becomes transparent. Set it aside to cool. Strain. Pour in wooden barrel. Add brewer's yeast. Cover with thick cloth and leave in warm place. When fermentation stops, close the barrel and leave in chilly place for 6-7 months. Then ladle into bottles, seal tightly and keep in cold place.

COFFEE WARSAW-STYLE
КАВА ПО-ВАРШАВСЬКОМУ

Brew coffee your favorite way in coffee maker or in pot using a little less water than usual. Add cream and sugar and bring to boil. Use ½ c. of cream or milk for making 1 c. coffee. Whip before serving.

OLD FASHIONED HONEY BEER
СТАРОДАВНЄ МЕДОВЕ ПИВО

10 lbs. honey
9 qts. water
1 T. beer yeast
½ bagel
½ t. hops
¼ t. cardamom
1/8 t. ground cloves

Dissolve honey in water and simmer on low heat until ½ of liquid evaporates. Set aside to cool. Add white bagel without crust soaked in 1 c. of water with dissolved brewing yeast. Add hops and let ferment. When it starts bubbling strongly, take out bread. Strain liquid in large container or barrel. Add cardamom and cloves tied in gauze. Nail up and leave in cold cellar for 12 days. Then open the barrel and take out gauze with spices. Ladle honey beer in 6 bottles. Seal and store for 2 months in cold place before using.

HOMEMADE HONEY BEER
МЕДОВЕ ПИВО ПО ДОМАШНЬОМУ

5 lbs. honey
3 qts. water
5 T. hops

Dissolve honey with water. Bring it to boil. Add hops and set in a chilly place. When fermentation stops, strain. Ladle in bottles and cork strongly.

KIEV-STYLE HONEY BEER
КИЇВСЬКЕ МЕДОВЕ ПИВО

6 lbs. honey
3 qts. water
7 T. hops
½ t. tea or ½ c. water

Mix honey with water. Cook for 3 hrs. Add hops tied in gauze with a little stone added in order to keep hops at bottom. Boil the mixture for 1 hr. Add water equal in amount to evaporated water and bring it to boil. Take of fire. Close with cover. Set aside to cool. Strain through cheesecloth into another vessel leaving about 10% head space. Store in warm place for 3-4 weeks until bubbling ends and fragrance of honey beer appears. Add strong tea and strain thoroughly. Ladle into bottles. Seal and store for half a year. The longer the beer is stored the better the taste becomes.

RECIPE INDEX

MENU TERMS

FOOD AND DRINK

The main thing to keep in mind with regard to the various foods and drinks listed in this chapter is their limited availability. Not everything will be available everywhere you go, so be prepared to experience new foods and methods of preparation. Most Ukrainian national dishes are very delicious.

Breakfast

Where can I have breakfast?	Де мо́жна посні́дати?	deh MOHZHnah pohSNEEdahtih
What time is breakfast served?	О котрі́й годи́ні сніда́нок?	oh KOHTreey gohDIHnee sneeDAHnohk
How late is breakfast served?	До котро́ї годи́ни мо́жна сніда́ти?	doh kohtROHyee goh-DIHnih MOHZHnah SNEEdahtih
I'd like...	Я хоті́в/ла би...	yah khohTEEV/lah bih
(black)	/чо́рну/	CHOHRnoo
coffee	ка́ву	KAHvoo
with milk	з молоко́м	z mohlohKOHM
with sugar	з цу́кром	z TSOOKrohm
without sugar	без цу́кру	behz TSOOKroo
tea	чай	chay
with lemon	з лимо́ном/ цитри́ною	z lihMOHnohm/ tsihTRIHnohyoo
with milk	з молоко́м	z mohlohKOHM
with honey	з ме́дом	z MEHdohm
with sugar	з цу́кром	z TSOOKrohm
cocoa	кака́о	kahKAHoh
milk	молоко́	mohlohKOH
juice	сік	seek
orange	апельси́новий	ahpehl'SIHnohvihy
grapefruit	грейпфру́товий	greypFROOtohvihy
tomato	тома́тний	tohMAHTnihy
kefir (a yogurt drink)	кефі́р	kehFEER
bread	хліб	khleeb
toast	грі́нки	GREENkih
a roll	бу́лочку	BOOlohchkoo
butter	ма́сло	MAHSloh

cheese	сир	sihr
pot cheese	сир	sihr
jam	повидло	pohVIHDloh
honey	мед	mehd
hot cereal	кашу	KAHshoo
hot buckwheat cereal	гречану кашу	grehCHAHnoo KAHshoo
hot rice cereal	рисову кашу	RIHsohvoo KAHshoo
farina	манну кашу	MAHNnoo KAHshoo
oatmeal	вівсяну кашу	veevSYAHnoo KAHshoo
eggs	яйця	YAYtsyah
scrambled eggs	омлет	ohmLEHT
a fried egg	яєшню	yaYEHSHnyoo
a boiled egg	варене яйце	vahREHneh YAYtseh
a hard boiled egg	круте яйце	krooTEH YAYtseh
salt/pepper	сіль/перець	seel'/PEHrehts'.

Appetizers

Ukrainian appetizers are quite hearty and may often seem like an entire meal onto themselves.

Appetizers	Закуски	zahKOOSkih
For an appetizer I want....	На закуску я хочу...	nah zahKOOSkoo yah KHOHchoo
(black/red) caviar	чорну/червону ікру	CHOHRnoo/chehrVOHnoo eekROO
cold, boiled pork with vegetables	буженину/ шинку з гарніром	boozhehNIHnoo/ SHIHNkoo z gahrNEErohm
cold roast beef with vegetables	ростбиф з гарніром	ROHSTbihf z gahrNEErohm
assorted meat/fish plate	асорті м'ясне/ рибне	ahsohrTEE myahsNEH/ RIHBneh
smoked/ pickled herring	копченого/ маринованого оселедця.	kohpCHEHnohgoh/ mahrihNOHvahnohgoh ohsehLEHDtsyah
meat/fish in aspic	заливне/ну м'ясо/рибу	zahlihvNEH/noo MYAHsoh/RIHboo
sausage	ковбасу	kohvbahSOO
sturgeon	осетрину	ohsehtRIHnoo

lox	сьомгу	SYOHMgoo
pancakes with...	млинці...	mlihnTSEE
caviar	з ікрою	z eekROHyoo
herring	з оселедцем	z ohsehLEHDtsehm
sour cream	зі сметаною	zee smehTAHnohyoo
jam	з варенням	z vahREHNnyahm
small pies filled with...	пиріжки...	pihreezhKIH
meat	з м'ясом	z MYAHsohm
cabbage	з капустою	z kahPOOStohyoo
rice	з рисом	z RIHsohm
potatoes	з картоплею	z kahrTOHPlehyoo
meat-filled dumplings	пельмені/вареники з м'ясом	pehlMEHnee/vahREHnihkih z MYAHsohm
marinated/salted mushrooms	мариновані/солені гриби	mahrihNOHvahnee/ sohLEHnee grihBIH
mushrooms baked in a sour cream sauce	жульєн з грибів	zhool'YEHN z grihBEEV
chicken baked in a sour cream sauce	жульєн з курчат	zhool'YEHN z koorCHAHT
Russian vegetable salad	вінігрет	veeneeGREHT
cucumber salad	салат з огірків	sahLAHT z ohgeerKEEV
tomato salad	салат з помідорів	sahLAHT z pohmeeDOHreev
cabbage salad	салат з капусти	sahLAHT z kahPOOStih
radish salad	салат з редиски	sahLAHT z rehDIHSkih
potato salad	картоплянний салат	kahrtohpLYAHnihy sahLAHT
meat salad	м'ясний салат	myahsNIHY sahLAHT
saurkraut	квашену капусту	KVAHshehnoo kahPOOStoo
liver pate	паштет з печінки	pahshTEHT z pehCHEENkih
olives	маслини	mahsLIHnih
radishes	редиску	rehDIHSkoo

Soups

For the first course I want...	На перше я хочу...	nah PEHRsheh yah KHOHchoo

Please bring me some...	Принесіть мені, будь ласка...	prihnehSEET' mehNEE bood'LAHSkah
borscht	борщ	bohrshch
boullion	бульйон	bool'YOHN
cabbage soup	капусняк	kahPOOSnyahk
chicken soup...	курячий суп...	KOOryachihy soop...
with noodles	з локшиною	z LOHKshihnohyoo
with rice	з рисом	z RIHsohm
cold kvas soup	окрошку	ohKROHSHkoo
cold vegetable soup	холодний борщ	khohLOHDnihy bohrshch
fish soup	рибна юшка	RIHBnah YOOSHkah
mushroom soup	грибний суп	grihbNIHY soop
pea soup	гороховий суп	gohROHkhohvihy soop
pickled cucumber soup	розсольник	rohzSOHL'nihk
potato soup	картопляний суп	kahrtohpLYAHnihy soop
spicy Georgian beef soup	харчо	khahrCHOH
tart meat/ fish soup	м'ясна/рибна солянка	myahsNAH/RIHBnah sohLYAHNkah
vegetable soup	овочевий суп	ohvohCHEHvihy soop

Grains and Cereals

I'd like...	Я хотів/ла би...	yah khohTEEV/lah bih
rice	рис	rihs
pilaf	плов	plohv
pasta	макарони	mahkahROHnih
potatoes	картоплю	kahrTOHPlyoo
fried	смажену	SMAHzhehnoo
boiled	варену	vahREHnoo
mashed	пюре	pyooREH
baked	печену	pehCHEHnoo
buckwheat	гречану кашу	grehCHAHnoo KAHshoo

Vegetables

What kind of vegetables are available?	Які у вас є овочі?	yahKEE oo vahs yeh OHvohchee
Cabbage	Капуста	kahPOOStah

299

Red cabbage	Брюссельська капуста	bryoosSEHL's'kah kahPOOStah
Beets	Буряки	booryahKIH
Tomatoes	Помідори	pohmeeDOHrih
Potatoes	Картопля	kahrTOHPlyah
Radishes	Редиска	rehDIHSkah
Cucumbers	Огірки	ohgeerKIH
Eggplant	Баклажани	bahklahZHAHnih
Mushrooms	Гриби	grihBIH
Peas	Горох	gohROHKH
Green beans	Квасоля	kvahSOHlyah
Wax beans	Спаржа	SPAHRzhah
Carrots	Морква	MOHRKvah
Onions	Цибуля	tsihBOOlyah
Leeks	Зелена цибуля	zehLehnah tsihBOOlyah
Corn	Кукурудза	kookooROODzah
Green peppers	Солодкий перець	sohLOHDkihy PEHrehts'
Red peppers	Червоний перець	chehrVOHnihy PEHrehts'
Parsley	Петрушка	pehtROOSHkah
Turnips	Ріпа	REEpah
Garlic	Часник	chahsNIHK
Cauliflower	Цвітна капуста	tsveetNAH kahPOOStah
Horseradish	Хрін	khreen

Preparations

How is this dish prepared?	Як готують цю страву?	yahk gohTOOyoot' tsyoo STRAHvoo
It's...	Вона...	vohNAH
baked	печена	pehCHEHnah
boiled	варена	vahREHnah
braised	тушкована	tooshKOHvahnah
breaded	запанірована	zahpahneeROHvahnah
chopped	посічена	pohSEEchehnah
fried	підсмажена	peedSMAHzhehnah
ground	перемелена	pehrehMEHlehnah
marinated	маринована	mahrihNOHvahnah
poached	відварена	veedVAHrehnah
raw	сира	sihRAH
roasted	засмажена	zahSMAHzhehnah
smoked	копчена	kohpCHEHnah
steamed	парова	pahrohVAH
stuffed	нафаршированa	nahfahrshihROHvahnah

Meat and Meat Dishes

For the second course I want...	На друге я хочу...	nah DROOgeh yah KHOHchoo
What kind of meat do you have?	Яке у вас є м'ясо?	yahKEH oo vahs yeh MYAHsoh
What kind of meat dishes do you have?	Які у вас є м'ясні страви?	yahKEE oo vahs yeh myahsNEE STRAHvih
Mutton	Бараннна	bahRAHnihnah
Lamb	Молода баранина	mohlohDAH bahRAHnihnah
Lamb chop	Бараняча відбивна	bahRAHnyahchah veedbihvNAH
Beef	Яловичина	yahlohVIHchihnah
Pork	Свинина	svihNIHnah
Pork chop	Свиняча відбивна	svihNYAHchah veedbihvNAH
Veal	Телятина	tehLYAHtihnah
Veal cutlet	Теляча відбивна	tehLYAHCHAH veedbihvNAH
Ham	Шинка	SHIHNkah
Roast beef	Ростбиф	ROHSTbihf
Pot roast	Тушкована яловичина	tooshKOHvahnah yahlohVIHchihnah
Meat patties	Битки	BIHTkih
Beefsteak	Біфштекс	beefSHTEHKS
Bacon	Корейка	kohREYkah
Meatloaf	М'ясний рулет	myahsNIHY rooLEHT
Meatballs	Тюфтелі	tyoofTEHlee
Sausages	Сосиски	sohSIHSkih
Shnitzel	Шніцель	SHNIHtsehl'
Meat stew	Рагу	rahGOO
Liver	Печінка	pehCHEENkah
Kidneys	Нирки	NIHRkih
Cutlet	Котлета відбивна	kohtLEHtah veedbihvNAH
Tongue	Язик	yahZIHK
Shish kebob	Шашлик	shahshLIHK
Ground lamb kebob	Люля-кебаб	lyooLYAH kehBAHB
Goulash	Гуляш	gooLYAHSH

Beef casserole	Душенина	dooshehNIHnah
Lamb stew	Азу	ahZOO
Chopped meat in a sauce	Смаженина	smahzhehNIHnah
Beef Stroganoff	Біфстроганов	beefSTROHgahnohv
Cabbage rolls with meat	Голубці	gohloobTSEE

Poultry and Game

What kind of poultry/ wild game dishes do you have?	Які у вас є страви з птицею і дичиною?	yahKEE oo vahs yeh STRAHvih z PTIHtsehyoo ee dihchihNOHyoo
Chicken	Курка	KOORkah
Duck	Качка	KAHCHkah
Goose	Гуска	GOOSkah
Turkey	Індик	eenDIHK
Woodcock	Вальдшнеп	vahl'dSHNEHP
Pigeon	Голуб	GOHloob
Hazel grouse	Рябчик	RYAHBchihk
Rabbit	Крілик	KREELihk
Hare	Заяць	ZAHyahts'
Venison	Оленина	ohlehNIHnah
Chicken Kiev	Котлети по-київськи	kohtLEHtih poh-KIHyihvs'kih
Georgian fried chicken	Курчата табака	koorCHAHtah tahbahKAH
Chicken cutlets	Пожарські котлети	pohZHAHRs'kee kohtLEHtih

Fish and Seafood

What kind of fish do you have?	Яка у вас є риба?	yahkah oo vahs yeh RIHbah
I'll take...	Я візьму...	yah veez'MOO
sturgeon	осетрину	ohsehtRIHnoo
pike-perch	судак	sooDAHK
trout	форель	fohREHL'
pike	щуку	SHCHOOkoo
flounder	камбалу	KAHMbahloo
carp	коропа	KOHrohpah
halibut	палтуса	PAHLtoosah

cod	тріску́	treesKOO
salmon	лососи́ну	lohsohSIHnoo
tuna	тунця́	toonTSYAH
herring	оселе́дця	ohsehLEHDtsyah
seafood	па́сту "Океа́н"	PAHStoo "OhkehAHN"
prawns	креве́тки	krehVEHTkih
crayfish	ра́ки	RAHkih
oysters	у́стриці	OOStrihtsee

Fruit

Some restaurants do not offer fresh fruit on their menus, but you may buy it at public markets, snack bars and kiosks.

What kind of fruit do you have?	Які у вас є фру́кти?	yahKEE oo vahs yeh FROOKtih
Is it fresh?	Вони́ сві́жі?	vohnih SVEEzhee
Apples	Я́блоки	YAHBlohkih
Oranges	Апельси́ни	ahpehl'SIHnih
Tangerines	Мандари́ни	mahndahRIHnih
Pears	Гру́ші	GROOshee
Peaches	Пе́рсики	PEHRsihkih
Plums	Сли́ви	SLIHvih
Melon	Ди́ня	DIHnyah
Watermelon	Каву́н	kahVOON
Bananas	Бана́ни	bahNAHnih
Apricots	Абрико́си	abrihKOHsih
Pineapple	Ананаси́	ahnahNAHsih
Grapes	Виногра́д	vihnohGRAHD
Raisins	Родзи́нки	rohDZIHNkih
Figs	і́нжир	eenZHIHR
Dates	Фі́ніки	FEEneekih
Lemon	Лимо́ни	lihMOHnih
Grapefruit	Грейпфру́ти	greypFROOtih
Prunes	Чорносли́в	chohrnohSLIHV
Currants	Порі́чки	pohREEchkih
Strawberries	Полуни́ці	pohlooNIHtsee
Wild strawberries	Суни́ці	sooNIHTsee
Cherries	Чере́шня	chehREHSHnyah
Blackberries	Ожи́на	ohZHIHnah
Cranberries	Клю́ква	KLYOOKvah
Raspberries	Мали́на	mahLIHnah
Blueberries	Чорни́ці	chohrNIHTsee

Dessert

Ukrainians claim that their ice cream, sold at kiosks year round, is the best in the world. Whether you agree or not, it is certainly worth a taste.

What do you have for dessert?	Що у вас є на десерт?	shchoh oo vahs yeh nah dehSEHRT
I'd like...	Я хотів/ла би...	yah khohTEEV/lah bih
ice cream	морозиво	mohROHzihvoh
a cookie	печиво	PEHchihvoh
pie	пиріг	pihREEG
pastry	тістечко	TEEStehchkoh
honey cake	медівник	mehdeevNIHK
cake	торт	tohrt
stewed fruit	компот	kohmPOHT
thin pancakes with jam	млинці з варенням	mlihnTSEE z vahREHNnyahm
thin fruit jelly	фруктове желе	frookTOHveh zhehLYEH
marzipan pastry	марципан	mahrtsihPAHN
filled doughnuts	пончики	POHNchihkih
an eclair	еклер	ehkLYEHR
chocolate	шоколад	shohkohLAHD
baked pudding	запіканку	zahpeeKAHNkoo

www.ingramcontent.com/pod-product-compliance
Lightning Source LLC
Jackson TN
JSHW011355130125
77033JS00023B/691

* 9 7 8 0 7 8 1 8 0 6 5 4 1 *